Uriah Furman Rogers

Jesus of Nazareth passeth by

The life of the Messiah

Uriah Furman Rogers

Jesus of Nazareth passeth by
The life of the Messiah

ISBN/EAN: 9783337257224

Printed in Europe, USA, Canada, Australia, Japan

Cover: Foto ©Lupo / pixelio.de

More available books at **www.hansebooks.com**

"I am come a light into the world, that whosoever believeth on me should not abide in darkness."

JESUS OF NAZARETH PASSETH BY

THE LIFE OF THE MESSIAH, COMPILED FROM THE AUTHORIZED VERSION OF THE FOUR GOSPELS.

ILLUSTRATED.

URIAH FURMAN ROGERS

Compiler and Publisher

EQUITABLE BUILDING
LETTER BOX 204
120 BROADWAY NEW YORK

Compiler's Preface.

NOT a few Christians—*fervent* believers in the vital significance of the sayings, doings and sufferings of the Lord Jesus Christ upon the earth—have a habit of mind and heart, as it were, of beholding, in sanctified imagination, the star that betokens their Lord's coming—of rejoicing with the shepherds—paying homage and presenting gifts with the wise men—accompanying Joseph, Mary and the "Child" into Egypt—returning with them to Nazareth—of listening to His wisdom in the temple—awaiting His return from the wilderness, and on to the end of His ministry accompanying Him, witnessing His miracles of infinite import, wrought through compassion and love—even to Gethsemane, and to the cross:

Thereafter, waiting at the tomb before the dawn with Mary called Magdalene—receiving His parting blessing with the first disciples, and with them seeing Him ascend to Heaven; where as the Son of man still, they behold Him, as did Stephen, at the right hand of God—the Redeemer of the human race from the curse of the Law, and the "One altogether lovely" who has secured eternal life for every mortal who wills to accept the unspeakable gift from His ever extended hand.

Dates, conjectural or positive, such believers think not of. To them a *chronological* record, though correct beyond dispute would seem of but little or no importance (in the circumstances of the case, and as is well understood, no

PREFACE.

such record is obtainable or can be determined). To these fervent souls it is enough that their Lord and Saviour, "in the fullness of time" became incarnate, accomplished His mission and returned from whence He came; where He ever liveth to intercede for all who believe and trust in Him, and who continuing, as yet, in this world of sin and sorrow, struggle and endure, until, touched by the finger of death, they find themselves in His glorious presence, with loved ones gone before, and with the redeemed and sanctified of all departed generations.

While to such believers an *illustrated* life of the Messiah is evidently no necessity, still to no Christians, as may well be thought, should such a work afford more pleasure—pleasure akin to that enjoyed by one who from personal associations has, and is taking his favorite and customary walk.

To that large wavering number who candidly confess that they do not really know whether they believe, or do not believe in Jesus of Nazareth as God manifest in the flesh, and the Saviour of the world—sometimes almost certain they do, and anon shake their heads as if again in doubt—inasmuch as it is with "the heart man believeth unto righteousness"—this work pictured as it is with incidents illustrating such meekness and patient suffering as were never exhibited by another in the history of mankind; and such love, so earnest that neither obloquy nor abandonment, nor the direst cruelty could cool much less extinguish—to the candid ones whom he now has in mind the compiler hopes and believes that his work will be

PREFACE.

both attractive and blessedly influential.

To agnostics who neither affirm nor deny the existence of a personal God, and who to the Christian, full of faith in the Lord Christ, seem almost to insist upon ignorance; and to their opposites, so to designate them, who profess to have found out God by thinking, or by special illumination as distinguished from the revelation recounted by the evangelists—to both of these classes this little work is recommended as a memento—containing as it does, in small compass, the details of that blessed "delusion" (if it be a delusion) that has given peace, hope and joy to many millions of human beings in the hour of dissolution of soul and body, and has been believed in and gratefully accepted as eternal truth, by a multitude of men distinguished for intellectual power, and for purity of heart and life, the world over.

The illustrations are reproductions of pictures by Murillo, Ribera, Louis Boullogne the elder, Rubens, Benjamin West P. R. A. Artland, W. Hamilton, R. A., Bird R. A., C. Landelle, Carrache Richard Cosway—R. A. Coypal, Guido, Bida, and other artists more or less distinguished for their representations of the person of the Saviour of mankind—the scenes in the midst of which He spent His life on earth, and the men, women and children with whom He mingled before His death on the cross, and after He arose triumphant from the grave.

U. F. R.

Nazareth [a Rose.]

INTRODUCTION

BEHOLD THE LAMB OF GOD WHICH TAKETH AWAY THE SIN OF THE WORLD.

JOHN THE BAPTIST.

JESUS OF NAZARETH
PASSETH BY.

CHAPTER I.

THE DIVINITY, HUMANITY AND OFFICE OF JESUS CHRIST.

IN the beginning was the Word, and the Word was with God, and the Word was God.

The same was in the beginning with God.

All things were made by Him; and without Him was not any thing made that was made..

In Him was life; and the life was the light of men.

And the light shineth in darkness; and the darkness comprehended it not.

¶ There was a man sent from God, whose name *was* John.

The same came for a witness, to bear witness of the Light, that all *men* through Him might believe.

He was not that Light, but *was sent* to bear witness of that Light.

That was the true Light, which lighteth every man that cometh into the world.

He was in the world, and the world was made by Him, and the world knew Him not.

He came unto His own,

and His own received Him not.

But as many as received Him, to them gave He power to become the sons of God, *even* to them that believe on His name:

Which were born, not of blood, nor of the will of the flesh, nor of the will of man, but of God.

And the Word was made flesh, and dwelt among us, (and we beheld His glory the glory as of the only begotten of the Father,) full of grace and truth.

¶ John bare witness of Him, and cried, saying, This was He of whom I spake, He that cometh after me is preferred before me.

And of His fullness have all we received, and grace for grace.

For the law was given by Moses, *but* grace and truth came by Jesus Christ.

No man hath seen God at any time; the only begotten Son, which is in the bosom of the Father, He hath declared *Him*.

THE ANNUNCIATION AND CONCEPTION OF JOHN THE BAPTIST.

¶ There was in the days of Herod, the king of Judea, a certain priest named Zacharias, of the course of Abia; and his wife *was* of the daughters of Aaron, and her name *was* Elisabeth.

And they were both righteous before God, walking in all the commandments and ordinances of the Lord blameless.

And they had no child, because that Elisabeth was barren; and they both were *now* well stricken in years.

And it came to pass, that, while he executed the priest's office before

The hill country of Judea.

God in the order of his course.

According to the custom of the priest's office, his lot was to burn incense when he went into the temple of the Lord.

And the whole multitude of the people were praying without at the time of incense.

And there appeared unto him an angel of the Lord standing on the right side of the altar of incense.

And when Zacharias saw *him* he was troubled and fear fell upon him.

But the angel said unto him, Fear not, Zacharias: for thy prayer is heard; and thy wife Elisabeth shall bear thee a son, and thou shalt call his name John.

And thou shalt have joy and gladness; and many shall rejoice at his birth.

For he shall be great in the sight of the Lord, and shall drink neither wine nor strong drink; and he shall be filled with the Holy Ghost, even from his mother's womb.

And many of the children of Israel shall he turn to the Lord their God.

And he shall go before Him in the spirit and power of Elias, to turn the hearts of the fathers to the children, and the disobedient to the wisdom of the just; to make ready a people prepared for the Lord.

And Zacharias said unto the angel, Whereby shall I know this? for I am an old man, and my wife well stricken in years.

And the angel answering said unto him, I am Gabriel, that stand in the presence of God; and am sent to speak unto thee, and to shew thee these glad tidings.

And, behold, thou shalt be dumb, and not able to speak, until the day that these things shall be performed, because thou believest not my words, which shall be fulfilled in their season.

And the people waited for Zacharias, and marvelled that he tarried so long in the temple.

And when he came out, he could not speak unto them: and they perceived that he had seen a vision in the temple; for he beckoned unto them and remained speechless.

And it came to pass, that, as soon as the days of his ministration were accomplished, he departed to his own house.

And after those days his wife Elisabeth conceived, and hid herself five months, saying,

Thus hath the Lord dealt with me in the days wherein he looked on *me* to take away my reproach among men.

THE ANNUNCIATION TO MARY.

AND in the sixth month the angel Gabriel was sent from God unto a city of Galilee, named Nazareth.

To a virgin espoused to a man whose name was Joseph, of the house of David; and the virgin's name *was* Mary.

And the angel came in unto her, and said, Hail, *thou that art* highly favored, the Lord *is* with thee: blessed *art* thou among women.

And when she saw *him* she was troubled at his saying, and cast in her mind what manner of salutation this should be.

And the angel said unto

And the angel said unto her, Fear not, Mary; for thou hast found favor with God.

her, Fear not, Mary; for thou hast found favor with God.

And, behold, thou shalt conceive in thy womb, and bring forth a son, and shalt call his name JESUS.

He shall be great, and shall be called the Son of the Highest; and the Lord God shall give unto Him the throne of His father David.

And He shall reign over the house of Jacob for ever; and of His kingdom there shall be no end.

Then said Mary unto the angel, How shall this be, seeing I know not a man?

And the angel answered and said unto her, The Holy Ghost shall come upon thee, and the power of the Highest shall overshadow thee; therefore also that holy thing which shall be born of thee shall be called the Son of God.

And, behold, thy cousin Elisabeth, she hath also conceived a son in her old age; and this is the sixth month with her, who was called barren.

For with God nothing shall be impossible.

And Mary said, Behold the handmaid of the Lord; be it unto me according to thy word. And the angel departed from her.

And Mary arose in those days, and went into the hill country with haste, into a city of Judea.

And entered into the house of Zacharias, and saluted Elisabeth.

And it came to pass, that, when Elisabeth heard the salutation of Mary, the babe leaped in her womb; and Elisabeth was filled with the Holy Ghost.

And she spake out with

a loud voice, and said, Blessed *as* thou among women, and blessed *is* the fruit of thy womb.

And whence *is* this to me, that the mother of my Lord should come to me?

For, lo, as soon as the voice of thy salutation sounded in mine ears, the babe leaped in my womb for joy.

And blessed *is* she that believed: for there shall be a performance of those things which were told her from the Lord.

And Mary said, My soul doth magnify the Lord.

And my spirit hath rejoiced in God my Savior.

For He hath regarded the low estate of His handmaiden: for behold, from henceforth all generations shall call me blessed.

For He that is mighty hath done to me great things; and holy *is* His name.

And His mercy *is* on them that fear Him from generation to generation.

He hath shewed strength with His arm; He hath scattered the proud in the imagination of their hearts.

He hath put down the mighty from *their* seats, and exalted them of low degree.

He hath filled the hungry with good things; and the rich He hath sent empty away.

He has holpen His servant Israel, in remembrance of *His* mercy.

As He spake to our fathers, to Abraham, and to his seed for ever.

And Mary abode with her about three months, and returned to her own house.

¶ Now Elizabeth's full time came that she should be

delivered; and she brought forth a son.

And her neighbors and her cousins heard how the Lord had shewed great mercy upon her; and they rejoiced with her.

And it came to pass, that on the eighth day they came to circumcise the child; and they called him Zacharias, after the name of his father.

And his mother answered and said, Not *so*: but he shall be called John.

And they said unto her: There is none of thy kindred that is called by this name.

And they made signs to his father, how he would have him called.

And he asked for a writing table, and wrote, saying, His name is John. And they marvelled all.

And his mouth was opened immediately, and his tongue *loosed*, and he spake and praised God.

And fear came on all that dwelt round about them: and all these sayings were noised abroad throughout all the hill country of Judea.

And all they that heard *them* laid *them* up in their hearts, saying, What manner of child shall this be! And the hand of the Lord was with him.

And his father Zacharias was filled with the Holy Ghost, and prophesied, saying,

Blessed *be* the Lord God of Israel; for He hath visited and redeemed His people,

And hath raised up a horn of salvation for us in the house of His servant David;

As He spake by the mouth of His holy prophets, which have been since the world began.

That we should be saved from our enemies, and from the hand of all that hate us ;

To perform the mercy *promised* to our fathers, and to remember His holy covenant.

The oath which He sware to our father Abraham,

That He would grant unto us, that we, being delivered out of the hands of our enemies, might serve Him without fear.

In holiness and righteousness before Him, all the days of our life.

And thou, child, shalt be called the prophet of the Highest: for thou shalt go before the face of the Lord to prepare His way ;

To give knowledge of salvation unto His people by the remission of their sins,

Through the tender mercy of our God ; whereby the day spring from on high hath visited us.

To give light to them that sit in darkness and *in* the shadow of death, to guide our feet into the way of peace.

And the child grew, and waxed strong in spirit, and was in the deserts till the day of his shewing unto Israel.

CHAPTER II.

THE INCARNATION OF CHRIST.

NOW the birth of Jesus Christ was on this wise: When as His mother Mary was espoused to Joseph, before they came together, she was found with child of the Holy Ghost.

Then Joseph her husband, being a *just* man, and not willing to make her a public example, was minded to put her away privily.

But while he thought on these things, behold, the

A Well at Nazareth.

angel of the Lord appeared unto him in a dream, saying, Joseph, thou son of David, fear not to take unto thee Mary thy wife: for that which is conceived in her is of the Holy Ghost.

And she shall bring forth a son, and thou shalt call His name JESUS: for He shall save His people from their sins.

Now all this was done, that it might be fulfilled which was spoken of the Lord by the prophet, saying,

"Behold, a virgin shall be with child, and bring forth a son, and they shall call His name Emanuel, which, being interpreted is, God with us.

Then Joseph being raised from sleep did as the angel of the Lord had bidden him, and took unto himself his wife.

And knew her not till she had brought forth her firstborn son: and he called His name JESUS.

And it came to pass in those days, that there went out a decree from Cæsar Augustus, that all the world should be taxed.

(*And* this taxing was first made when Cyrenius was governor of Syria.)

And all went to be taxed, every one into his own city.

And Joseph also went up from Galilee, out of the city of Nazareth, into Judea, unto the city of David, which is called Bethlehem, (because he was of the house and lineage of David.)

To be taxed with Mary, his expoused wife, being great with child.

And so it was, that, while they were there, the days were accomplished that she should be delivered.

And she brought forth her first born son, and wrapped Him in swaddling clothes and laid Him in a manger; because there was no room for them in the inn.

And there were in the same country shepherds abiding in the field, keeping watch over their flock by night.

And, lo, the angel of the Lord came unto them, and the glory of the Lord shone round about them; and they were sore afraid.

And the angel said unto them, Fear not; for, behold, I bring you tidings of great joy, which shall be to all people.

For unto you is born this day in the city of David a Saviour, which is Christ the Lord.

And this *shall be* a sign unto you; Ye shall find the babe wrapped in swaddling clothes, lying in a manger.

And suddenly there was with the angel a multitude of the heavenly host praising God, and saying,

Glory to God in the highest, and on earth peace, good will toward men.

And it came to pass, as the angels were gone away from them into heaven, the shepherds said one to another, Let us now go even unto Bethlehem, and see this thing which is come to pass, which the Lord has made known unto us.

And they came with haste and found Mary and Joseph, and the babe lying in a manger.

And when they had seen *it*, they made known abroad the saying which was told them, concerning this child.

And all they that heard *it* wondered at those things which were told them by the shepherds.

But Mary kept all these

And they came with haste.

things, and pondered *them* in her heart.

And the shepherds returned, gloryifying and praising God for all the things that they had heard and seen, as it was told unto them.

And when eight days were accomplished for the circumcising of the child, His name was called JESUS, which was so named of the angel before He was conceived in the womb.

And when the days of her purification according to the law of Moses were accomplished, they brought Him to Jerusalem, to present *Him* to the Lord.

(As it is written in the law of the Lord, Every male that openeth the womb shall be called holy to the Lord ;)

And to offer a sacrifice according to that which is said in the law of the Lord,
"A pair of turtledoves, or two young pigeons."

SIMEON.

AND, behold, there was a man in Jerusalem, whose name *was* Simeon ; and the same man *was* just and devout, waiting for the consolation of Israel ; and the Holy Ghost, was upon him.

And it was revealed unto him by the Holy Ghost, that he should not see death, before he had seen the Lord's Christ.

And he came by the Spirit into the temple ; and when the parents brought in the child Jesus, to do for Him after the custom of the law,

Then took he Him up in his arms, and blessed God, and said,

Lord, now lettest thy servant depart in peace, according to thy word :

For mine eyes have seen thy salvation,

Which thou hast prepared before the face of all people;

A light to lighten the Gentiles, and the glory of thy people Israel.

And Joseph and His mother marveled at those things which were spoken of Him.

And Simeon blessed them, and said unto Mary His Mother, Behold, this *child* is set for the fall and rising again of many in Israel; and for a sign which shall be spoken against;

(Yea, a sword shall pierce through thy own soul also;) that the thoughts of many hearts may be revealed.

ANNA.

AND there was one Anna, a prophetess, the daughter of Phanuel, of the tribe of Aser; she was of great age, and had lived with an husband seven years from her virginity;

And she *was* a widow of about fourscore and four years, which departed not from the temple, but served *God* with fastings and prayers night and day.

And she coming in that instant gave thanks likewise unto the Lord, and spake of Him to all them that looked for redemption in Jerusalem.

CHAPTER III.

THE STAR IN THE EAST

NOW when Jesus was born in Bethlehem of Judea in the days of Herod the king, behold, there came wise men from the east to Jerusalem,

Saying, Where is He that is born King of the Jews? for we have seen His star in the east, and are come to worship Him.

When Herod the king had heard *these things* he

The Star in the East.

THE WISE MEN WORSHIP THE CHILD, AND PRESENT UNTO HIM GIFTS.

was troubled, and all Jerusalem with him.

And when he had gathered all the chief priests and scribes of the people together, he demanded of them where Christ should be born.

And they said unto him, In Bethlehem of Judea: for thus it is written by the prophet,

"And thou Bethlehem, *in* the land of Juda, art not the least among the princes of Juda, for out of thee shall come a Governor that shall rule my people Israel."

Then Herod, when he had privily called the wise men, inquired of them diligently what time the star appeared.

And he sent them to Bethlehem, and said, Go and search diligently for the young child: and when ye have found *Him*, bring me the word again, that I may come and worship Him also.

When they had heard the king, they departed; and lo, the star which they saw in the east, went before them, till it came and stood over where the young child was.

When they saw the star they rejoiced with exceeding great joy.

And when they had come into the house, they saw the young child with Mary His mother, and fell down and worshipped Him: and when they had opened their treasures, they presented unto Him gifts; gold, and frankincense, and myrrh.

And being warned of God in a dream that they should not return to Herod, they departed into their own country another way.

And when they were departed, behold, the angel of the Lord appeared to

Joseph in a dream, saying, Arise, and take the young child and His mother and flee into Egypt, and be thou there until I bring thee word: for Herod will seek the young child to destroy Him.

When he arose, he took the young child and his mother by night; and departed into Egypt.

And was there until the death of Herod: that it might be fulfilled which was spoken of the Lord by the prophet, saying, "Out of Egypt have I called my son."

Then Herod, when he saw that he was mocked of the wise men, was exceeding worth, and sent forth, and slew all the children that were in Bethlehem, and in all the coasts thereof, from two years old and under, according to the time which he had diligently inquired of the wise men.

Then was fulfilled that which was spoken by Jeremy the prophet, saying,

In Rama was there a voice heard, lamentation, and weeping, and great mourning, Rachel weeping *for* her children, and would not be comforted, because they are not.

But when Herod was dead, behold, an angel of the Lord appeareth in a dream to Joseph in Egypt,

Saying, Arise, and take the young child and His mother, and go into the land of Israel.

But when he heard that Archelaus did reign in Judea in the room of his father Herod, he was afraid to go thither: notwithstanding, being warned of God in a dream, he turned aside into the parts of Galilee:

And he came and dwelt

The departure into Egypt.

"In Rama was there a voice heard, lamentation, and weeping, and great mourning."

"Out of Egypt have I called My Son."

"He shall be called a Nazarene."

And all that heard Him were astonished at His understanding and answers.

And He went down with them, and came to Nazareth, and was subject unto them: but His mother kept all these sayings in her heart.

in a city called Nazareth; that it might be fulfilled which was spoken by the prophets, "He shall be called a Nazarene."

And the child grew, and waxed strong in spirit, filled with wisdom; and the grace of God was upon Him.

Now His parents went to Jerusalem every year at the feast of the passover.

And when He was twelve years old, they went up to Jerusalem after the custom of the feast.

And when they had fulfilled the days, and as they returned, the child Jesus tarried behind in Jerusalem and Joseph and His mother knew not *of it.*

But they, supposing Him to have been in the company, went a day's journey; and they sought Him among *their* kinsfolk and acquaintance.

And when they found Him not, they turned back again to Jerusalem, seeking Him.

And it came to pass, that after three days they found Him in the temple, sitting in the midst of the doctors, both hearing them, and asking them questions.

And all that heard Him were astonished at His understanding and answers.

And when they saw Him, they were amazed; and His mother said unto Him, Son, why hast thou thus dealt with us? behold, thy father and I have sought thee sorrowing.

And He said unto them, How is it that ye sought me? wist ye not that I must be about my Father's business?

And they understood not the saying which He spake unto them.

And He went down with them, and came to Nazareth, and was subject unto them; but His mother kept all these sayings in her heart.

And Jesus increased in wisdom and stature, and in favour with God and man.

CHAPTER IV.

JOHN THE BAPTIST.

NOW in the fifteenth year of the reign of Tiberius Cæsar, Pontius Pilate, being governor of Judea, and Herod being tetrarch of Galilee, and his brother Philip tetrarch of Iturea and of the region of Trachonitis, and Lysanias the tetrarch of Abilene.

Annas and Caiaphas being the high priests, the word of God came unto John the son of Zacharias in the wilderness.

And he came into all the country about Jordan, preaching the baptism of repentance for the remission of sins; saying, Repent ye; for the kingdom of heaven is at hand.

For this is He who was spoken of by the prophet Esaias, saying, "The voice of one crying in the wilderness, Prepare ye the way of the Lord, make His paths straight.

"Every valley shall be filled, and every mountain and hill shall be brought low; and the crooked shall be made straight, and the rough ways *shall be* made smooth;

"And all flesh shall see the salvation of God."

And the same John had his raiment of camel's hair, and a leathern girdle about his loins; and his meat was locusts and wild honey.

And there went out unto him all the land of Judea, and they of Jerusalem, and

"The Voice of one crying in the wilderness."

all the region round about Jordan, and were all baptized of him in the river of Jordan, confessing their sins.

But when he saw many of the Pharisees and Sadducees come to his baptism, he said unto them, O generation of vipers, who hath warned you to flee from the wrath to come?

Bring forth therefore fruits meet for repentance:

And think not to say within yourselves, we have Abraham to *our* father: for I say unto you, that God is able of these stones to raise up children unto Abraham.

And now also the axe is laid unto the root of the trees: therefore every tree which bringeth not forth good fruit is hewn down and cast into the fire.

And the people asked him, saying, What shall we do then?

He answereth and saith unto them, He that hath two coats, let him impart to him that hath none; and he that hath meat, let him do likewise.

Then came also publicans to be baptized, and said unto him, Master, what shall we do?

And he said unto them, Exact no more than that which is appointed you.

And the soldiers likewise demanded of him, saying, And what shall we do? And he said unto them, Do violence to no man, neither accuse *any* falsely; and be content with your wages.

And as the people were in expectation, and all men mused in their hearts of John, whether he were the Christ, or not;

John answered, saying unto *them* all, I indeed baptize you with water unto repentance; but there cometh one mightier than I after me, the latchet of whose shoes I am not worthy to stoop down and unloose.

I indeed have baptized you with water: but He shall baptize you with the Holy Ghost, and *with* fire.

Whose fan *is* in His hand, and He will thoroughly purge His floor, and gather His wheat into the garner; but He will burn up the chaff with unquenchable fire.

And many other things in his exhortation preached he unto the people.

CHAPTER V.

THE BAPTISM AND TEMPTATION OF JESUS.

AND Jesus himself began to be about thirty years of age, being (as was supposed) the son of Joseph.

Then cometh Jesus from Galilee to Jordan unto John, to be baptized of him.

But John forbade Him, saying, I have need to be baptized of thee, and comest thou to me?

And Jesus answering said unto him, Suffer *it to be so* now: for thus it becometh us to fulfil all righteousness. Then he suffered Him.

And Jesus, when He was baptized, went up straightway out of the water: and, lo, the heavens were opened unto Him, and He saw the Spirit of God descending like a dove, and lighting upon Him:

And lo a voice from heaven, saying, this is my beloved Son, in whom I am well pleased.

And Jesus being full of the Holy Ghost returned from Jordan, and was led by the Spirit into the wilderness.

Being forty days tempted

The Temptation.

of the devil. And in those days He did eat nothing: and when they were ended, He afterward hungered.

And the devil said unto Him, If thou be the Son of God, command this stone that it be made bread.

And Jesus answered him, saying, It is written, That man shall not live by bread alone, but by every word of God.

And the devil, taking Him up into a high mountain, shewed unto him all the kingdoms of the world in a moment of time.

And the devil said unto Him, All this power will I give thee, and the glory of them; for that is delivered unto me; and to whomsoever I will, I give it.

If thou therefore wilt worship me, all shall be thine.

And Jesus answered and said unto him, Get thee behind me, Satan: for it is written, Thou shalt worship the Lord thy God, and Him only shalt thou serve.

And he brought Him to Jerusalem, and set Him on a pinnacle of the temple, and said unto Him, If thou be the Son of God, cast thyself down from hence:

For it is written, He shall give His angels charge over thee, to keep thee:

And in *their* hands they shall bear thee up, lest at any time thou dash thy foot against a stone.

And Jesus answering said unto him, It is said, Thou shalt not tempt the Lord thy God.

And when the devil had ended all the temptation, he departed from Him for a season, and, behold, angels came and ministered unto Him.

From that time Jesus began to preach, and to

say, Repent, for the kingdom of heaven is at hand.

¶ In those days John did baptize in the wilderness, and bare witness of Him, and cried, saying, This was He of whom I spake, He that cometh after me is preferred before me; for He was before me.

And of His fulness have all we received, and grace for grace.

For the law was given by Moses, *but* grace and truth came by Jesus Christ.

No man hath seen God at any time; the only begotten Son, which is in the bosom of the Father, He hath declared *Him*.

And this is the record of John, when the Jews sent priests and Levites from Jerusalem to ask him, Who art thou?

And he confessed and denied not; but confessed, I am not the Christ.

And they asked him, What then? Art thou Elias? And he saith, I am not. Art thou that Prophet? And he answered, No.

Then said they unto him, Who art thou? that we may give an answer to them that sent us. What sayest thou of thyself?

He said, I *am* "the voice of one crying in the wilderness, Make straight the way of the Lord?" as said the prophet Esaias.

And they which were sent were of the Pharisees; and they asked him, and said unto him, why baptizest thou then, if thou be not that Christ, nor Elias, neither that Prophet?

John answered them, saying, I baptize with water: but there standeth one among you, whom ye know

Then the devil leaveth Him, and, behold, angels came and ministered unto Him.

not: He it is, who coming after me is preferred before me, whose shoe's latchet I am not worthy to unloose.

These things were done in Bethabara beyond Jordan, where John was baptizing.

The next day John seeth Jesus coming unto him, and saith, behold the Lamb of God, which taketh away the sin of the world!

This is He of whom I said, After me cometh a man which is preferred before me; for He was before me.

And I knew Him not: but that He should be made manifest to Israel, therefore am I come baptizing with water.

And John bare record, saying, I saw the Spirit descending from heaven like a dove, and it abode upon Him.

And I knew Him not: but He that sent me to baptize with water, the same said unto me, Upon whom thou shalt see the Spirit descending, and remaining on Him, the same is He which baptizeth with the Holy Ghost.

And I saw, and bare record that this is the Son of God.

Again the next day after, John stood, and two of his disciples:

And looking upon Jesus as He walked, he saith, Behold the Lamb of God!

And the two disciples heard him speak, and they followed Jesus.

Then Jesus turned, and saw them following, and saith unto them, What seek ye? They said unto Him, Rabbi, (which is to say, being interpreted, Master) where dwellest thou?

He saith unto them,

Come and see. They came and saw where He dwelt, and abode with Him that day; for it was about the tenth hour.

One of the two which heard John *speak*, and followed Him, was Andrew, Simon Peter's brother.

He first findeth his own brother Simon, and saith unto him, We have found the Messiah, which is, being interpreted, the Christ.

And he brought him to Jesus. And when Jesus beheld him, He said, Thou art Simon, the son of Jona: thou shalt be called Cephas, which is by interpretation, a stone.

¶ The day following Jesus would go forth into Galilee, and findeth Philip, and saith unto him, Follow me.

Now Philip was of Bethsaida, the city of Andrew and Peter.

Philip findeth Nathanael, and saith unto him, We have found Him, of whom Moses in the law, and the prophets, did write, Jesus of Nazareth, the son of Joseph.

And Nathanael said unto him, Can there any good thing come out of Nazareth? Philip saith unto him, Come and see.

Jesus saw Nathanael coming to Him, and saith of him, Behold an Israelite indeed, in whom is no guile!

Nathanael saith unto Him, Whence knowest thou me? Jesus answered and said unto him, Before that Philip called thee, when thou wast under the fig tree, I saw thee.

Nathanael answered and saith unto Him, Rabbi, thou art the King of Israel.

Jesus answered and said

This beginning of miracles did Jesus in Cana of Galilee.

unto him, Because I said unto thee, I saw thee under the fig tree, believest thou? thou shalt see greater things than these.

And he saith unto him, Verily, verily, I say unto you, Hereafter ye shall see heaven open, and the angels of God ascending and descending upon the Son of Man.

CHAPTER VI.

CHRIST AT THE MARRIAGE FEAST IN CANA.

AND the third day there was a marriage in Cana of Galilee: and the mother of Jesus was there:

And both Jesus was called, and His disciples to the marriage.

And when they wanted wine, the mother of Jesus saith unto Him, They have no wine.

Jesus saith unto her, Woman, what have I to do with thee? mine hour is not yet come.

His mother saith unto the servants, Whatsoever He saith unto you, do *it*.

And there were set there six water-pots of stone, after the manner of the purifying of the Jews, containing two or three firkins apiece.

Jesus saith unto them, Fill the water-pots with water, and they filled them up to the brim.

And He saith unto them, Draw out now, and bear unto the governor of the feast. And they bare *it*.

When the ruler of the feast had tasted the water that was made wine, and knew not whence it was, (but the servants which drew the water knew,) the governor of the feast called the bridegroom,

And saith unto him, Every man at the beginning doth set forth good wine; and when men have well drunk, then that which is worse: *but* thou has kept the good wine until now.

This beginning of miracles did Jesus in Cana of Galilee, and manifested forth His glory; and His disciples believed on Him.

CLEARS THE TEMPLE.

¶ AFTER this He went down to Capernaum, He, and His mother, and His brethren, and His disciples; and they continued there not many days.

And the Jews' passover was at hand, and Jesus went up to Jerusalem,

And found in the temple those that sold oxen and sheep and doves, and the changers of money sitting:

And when He had made a scourge of small cords, He drove them all out of the temple, and the sheep, and the oxen; and poured out the changers' money, and overthrew the tables;

And said unto them that sold doves, Take these things hence; make not my Father's house a house of merchandise.

And His disciples remembered that it was written, The zeal of thine house hath eaten me up.

Then answered the Jews and said unto Him, What sign shewest thou unto us, seeing that thou doest these things?

Jesus answered and said unto them, Destroy this temple, and in three days I will raise it up.

Then said the Jews, Forty and six years was this temple in building, and wilt thou rear it up in three days?

But He spake of the temple of His body.

When therefore He was

"Take these things hence; make not my Father's house a house of merchandise."

risen from the dead, His disciples remembered that He had said this unto them ; and they believed the Scripture, and the word which Jesus had said.

Now, when He was in Jerusalem at the passover, in the feast-*day*, many believed in His name, when they saw the miracles which He did.

But Jesus did not commit himself unto them, because He knew all *men*,

And needed not that any should testify of man : for He knew what was in man.

THE NEW BIRTH.

There was a man of the Pharisees, named Nicodemus, a ruler of the Jews :

The same came to Jesus by night, and said unto Him, Rabbi, we know that thou art a teacher come from God : for no man can do these miracles that thou doest, except God be with him.

Jesus answered and said unto him, Verily, verily, I say unto thee, Except a man be born again, he cannot see the kingdom of God.

Nicodemus said unto Him How can a man be born when he is old ? can he enter the second time into his mother's womb and be born ?

Jesus answered, Verily, verily, I say unto thee, Except a man be born of water and *of* the Spirit, he cannot enter into the kingdom of God.

That which is born of the flesh is flesh ; and that which is born of the Spirit is spirit.

Marvel not that I said unto thee, Ye must be born again.

The wind bloweth where it listeth, and thou hearest

the sound thereof, but canst not tell whence it cometh, and whither it goeth: so is every one that is born of the Spirit.

Nicodemus answered and said unto Him, How can these things be?

Jesus answered and said unto him, Art thou a master of Israel, and knowest not these things?

Verily, verily, I say unto thee, We speak that we do know, and testify that we have seen; and ye receive not our witness.

If I have told you earthly things, and ye believe not, how shall ye believe, if I tell you *of* heavenly things?

And no man hath ascended up to heaven, but He that came down from heaven, *even* the Son of man which is in heaven.

And as Moses lifted up the serpent in the wilderness even so must the Son of man be lifted up:

That whosoever believeth in Him should not perish, but have eternal life.

For God so loved the world, that He gave His only begotten Son, that whosoever believeth in Him should not perish, but have everlasting life.

For God sent not His Son into the world to condemn the world; but that the world through Him might be saved.

He that believeth on Him is not condemned: but he that believeth not is condemned already, because He hath not believed in the name of the only begotten Son of God.

And this is the condemnation, that light has come into the world, and men loved darkness rather than light, because their deeds were evil.

For every one that doeth evil hateth the light, neither cometh to the light, lest his deeds should be reproved.

But he that doeth truth cometh to the light, that his deeds may be made manifest, that they are wrought in God.

¶ After these things came Jesus and His disciples into the land of Judea; and there He tarried with them, and baptized.

And John also was baptizing in Enon near to Salim, because there was much water there: and they came and were baptized.

For John was not yet cast into prison.

Then there arose a question between *some* of John's disciples and the Jews about purifying.

And they came unto John, and said unto him, Rabbi, He that was with thee beyond Jordan, to whom thou bearest witness, behold, the same baptizeth, and all *men* come to Him.

John answered and said, A man can receive nothing, except it be given him from heaven.

Ye yourselves bear me witness, that I said, I am not the Christ, but that I am sent before Him.

He that hath the bride is the bridegroom: but the friend of the bridegroom, which standeth and heareth him, rejoiceth greatly because of the bridegroom's voice: this my joy therefore is fulfilled.

He must increase, but I *must* decrease.

He that cometh from above is above all: he that is of the earth is earthly, and speaketh of the earth: He that cometh from heaven is above all.

And what He hath seen and heard, that He testifieth; and no man receiveth His testimony.

He that hath received His testimony hath set to his seal that God is true.

For He whom God hath sent speaketh the words of God: for God giveth not the Spirit by measure *unto Him.*

The Father loveth the Son, and hath given all things into His hand.

He that believeth on the Son hath everlasting life: and he that believeth not the Son shall not see life; but the wrath of God abideth on him.

CHAPTER VII.

IN SAMARIA AND GALILEE.

HEROD the tetrarch, being reproved by John for Herodias his brother Philip's wife, and for all the evils which Herod had done, added yet this above all, that he shut up John in prison.

When therefore the Lord knew how the Pharisees had heard that Jesus made and baptized more disciples than John,

(Though Jesus Himself baptized not, but His disciples,) and had heard that John was cast into prison,

He left Judea, and departed again into Galilee.

And He must needs go through Samaria.

Then cometh He to a city of Samaria, which is called Sychar, near to the parcel of ground that Jacob gave to his son Joseph.

Now Jacob's well was there. Jesus, therefore, being wearied with *His* journey, sat thus on the well: *and* it was about the sixth hour.

There cometh a woman

Then cometh He to a city of Samaria, which is called Sychar.

of Samaria to draw water: Jesus saith unto her, Give me to drink.

(For His disciples were gone away unto the city to buy meat.)

Then saith the woman of Samaria unto Him, How is it that thou, being a Jew, asketh drink of me, which am a woman of Samaria? for the Jews have no dealings with the Samaritans.

Jesus answered and said unto her, If thou knewest the gift of God, and who it is that saith to thee, Give me to drink; thou wouldest have asked of Him, and He would have given thee living water.

The woman saith unto Him, Sir, thou hast nothing to draw with, and the well is deep: from whence then hast thou that living water?

Art thou greater than our father Jacob, which gave us the well, and drank thereof himself, and his children, and his cattle?

Jesus answered and said unto her, Whosoever drinketh of this water shall thirst again:

But whosoever drinketh of the water that I shall give him shall never thirst; but the water that I shall give him shall be in him a well of water springing up into everlasting life.

The woman said unto Him Sir, give me this water, that I thirst not, neither come hither to draw.

Jesus saith unto her, Go, call thy husband, and come hither.

The woman answered and said, I have no husband. Jesus said unto her, Thou hast well said, I have no husband:

For thou hast had five husbands; and he whom thou now hast is not thy husband: in that saidst thou truly.

The woman said unto Him, Sir, I perceive that thou art a prophet.

Our fathers worshipped in this mountain; and ye say, that in Jerusalem is the place where men ought to worship.

Jesus said unto her, Woman, believe me, the hour cometh, when ye shall neither in this mountain, nor yet at Jerusalem, worship the Father.

Ye worship ye know not what: we know what we worship; for salvation is of the Jews.

But the hour cometh, and now is, when the true worshippers shall worship the Father in spirit and in truth: for the Father seeketh such to worship Him.

God *is* a Spirit: and they that worship Him must worship *Him* in spirit and in truth.

The woman saith unto Him, I know that Messias cometh, which is called Christ: when He is come, He will tell us all things.

Jesus saith unto her, I that speak unto thee am *He.*

And upon this came His disciples, and marvelled that He talked with the woman: yet no man said, What seekest thou? or, Why talkest thou with her?

The woman then left her water-pot, and went her way into the city, and saith to the men,

Come, see a man which told me all things that ever I did: is not this the Christ?

Then they went out of the city, and came unto Him.

In the meanwhile His disciples prayed Him, saying, Master, eat.

"God *is* a Spirit: and they that worship Him must worship *Him* in spirit and in truth."

But He said unto them, I have meat to eat that ye know not of.

Therefore said the disciples one to the other, Hath any man brought Him *aught* to eat?

Jesus saith unto them, My meat is to do the will of Him that sent me, and to finish His work.

Say not ye, There are yet four months, and *then* cometh harvest? behold, I say unto you, Lift up your eyes, and look on the fields; for they are white already to harvest.

And he that reapeth receiveth wages, and gathereth fruit unto life eternal: that both he that soweth and he that reapeth may rejoice together.

And herein is that saying true, One soweth, and another reapeth.

I sent you to reap that whereon ye bestowed no labour: other men laboured, and ye are entered into their labours.

And many of the Samaritans of that city believed on Him for the saying of the woman, which testified, He told me all-things that ever I did.

So when the Samaritans were come unto Him, they besought Him that He would tarry with them: and He abode there two days.

And many more believed because of His own word;

And said unto the woman, Now we believe, not because of thy saying: for we have heard *Him* ourselves, and know that this is indeed the Christ, the Saviour of the world.

¶ Now after two days He departed thence, and went into Galilee.

For Jesus himself testified

that a prophet hath no honour in his own country.

Then when He was come into Galilee, the Galileans received Him, having seen all the things that He did at Jerusalem at the feast: for they also went unto the feast.

So Jesus came again into Cana of Galilee, where He made the water wine. And there was a certain nobleman, whose son was sick at Capernaum.

When he heard that Jesus was come out of Judea into Galilee, he went unto Him, and besought Him that he would come down, and heal his son; for he was at the point of death.

Then said Jesus unto him, Except ye see signs and wonders, ye will not believe.

The nobleman saith unto Him, Sir, come down ere my child die.

Jesus saith unto him, Go thy way; thy son liveth. And the man believed the word that Jesus had spoken unto him, and he went his way.

And as he was now going down, his servants met him, and told *him*, saying, Thy son liveth.

Then inquired he of them the hour when he began to amend. And they said unto him, Yesterday at the seventh hour the fever left him.

So the father knew that *it was* at the same hour, in the which Jesus said unto him, Thy son liveth: and himself believed, and his whole house.

This *is* again the second miracle *that* Jesus did, when He was come out of Judea into Galilee.

And He taught in their synagogues, being glorified of all.

CHAPTER VIII.

HE BEGINNETH TO PREACH

AND Jesus returned in the power of the Spirit into Galilee: and there went out a fame of Him through all the region round about.

And He taught in their synagogues, being glorified of all.

And He came to Nazareth where He had been brought up: and as His custom was, He went into the synagogue on the sabbath day, and stood up for to read.

And there was delivered unto Him the book of the prophet Esaias. And when He had opened the book, He found the place where it was written,

"The spirit of the Lord *is* upon me, because He hath anointed me to preach the gospel to the poor: He hath sent me to heal the broken-hearted, to preach deliverance to the captives, and recovering of sight to the blind, to set at liberty them that are bruised.

"To preach the acceptable year of the Lord."

And He closed the book, and He gave *it* again to the minister, and sat down. and the eyes of all them that were in the synagogue were fastened on Him.

And He began to say unto them, This day is this Scripture fulfilled in your ears.

And all bear Him witness, and wondered at the gracious words which proceeded out of His mouth.

And were astonished, saying, From whence hath this *man* these things? and what wisdom *is* this which is given unto Him, that even such mighty works are wrought by His hands?

And they said, Is not this the carpenter? is not this Joseph's son? the son of Mary, the brother of James, and Joses, and of Juda, and Simon? and are not His sisters here with us? Whence then hath this *man* all these things? And they were offended in Him.

But Jesus said unto them, A prophet is not without honour, but in his own country, and among his own kin, and in his own house.

(And He could there do no mighty work, because of their unbelief, save that He laid His hands upon a few sick folk, and healed *them*. And He marvelled because of their unbelief.)

And He said unto them, Ye will surely say unto me this proverb, Physician, heal thyself: whatsoever we have heard done in Capernaum, do also here in thy country.

And He said, Verily, I say unto you, No prophet is accepted in his own country.

But I tell you of a truth, many widows were in Israel in the days of Elias, when the heaven was shut up three years and six months, when great famine was throughout all the land.

But unto none of them was Elias sent, save unto Sarepta, *a city* of Sidon, unto a woman *that was* a widow.

And many lepers were in Israel in the time of Eliseus the prophet: and none of them was cleansed, saving Naaman the Syrian.

And all they in the synagogue, when they heard these things, were filled with wrath.

And rose up, and thrust

But He, passing through the midst of them, went His way.

Him out of the city, and led Him unto the brow of the hill whereon their city was built, that they might cast Him down headlong.

But He, passing through the midst of them, went His way, and came and dwelt in Capernaum, a city of Galilee, which is upon the sea coast, in the borders of Zebulon and Nephthalim, and taught them on the Sabbath days.

That it might be fulfilled which was spoken by Esaias the prophet, saying,

"The land of Zebulon, and the land of Nephthalim, *by* the way of the sea, beyond Jordan, Galilee of the Gentiles;

"The people which sat in darkness saw great light; and to them which sat in the region and shadow of death, light is sprung up."

And they were astonished at His doctrine; for His word was with power.

¶ And Jesus, walking by the sea of Galilee, saw Simon called Peter, and Andrew his brother, casting a net into the sea; for they were fishers.

And He saith unto them, Come ye after me, and I will make you to become fishers of men. And straightway they forsook their nets, and followed Him.

And going on from thence, He saw James *the son* of Zebedee, and John his brother, in a ship with Zebedee their father, mending their nets;

And straightway He called them : and they immediately left the ship and their father Zebedee in the ship with the hired servants, and went after Him.

And they went into Capernaum; and straightway on the sabbath day He entered into the synagogue, and taught.

And they were astonished at His doctrine: for He taught them as one that had authority, and not as the scribes.

HE CASTETH OUT DEVILS

AND in the synagogue there was a man, which had a spirit of an unclean devil, and cried out with a loud voice,

Saying, Let *us* alone; what have we to do with thee, *thou* Jesus of Nazareth? art thou come to destroy us? I know Thee who thou art, the holy one of God.

And Jesus rebuked him, saying, Hold thy peace, and come out of him.

And when the unclean spirit had thrown him in the midst, and had torn him, and cried with a loud voice, he came out of him, and hurt him not.

And they were all amazed, and spake among themselves, saying, What a word *is* this! for with authority and power He commanded the unclean spirits, and they come out.

And the fame of Him went out into every place of the country round about.

And He arose out of the synagogue, and entered into Simon's house. And Simon's wife's mother was taken with a great fever; and they besought Him for her.

And He stood over her, and rebuked the fever; and it left her: and immediately she arose and ministered unto them.

Now when the sun was setting, all they that had any sick with divers diseases brought them unto

"Come ye after Me, and I will make you to become fishers of men."

And He laid His hands on every one of them, and healed them; and devils also came out of many.

And in the morning, rising up a great while before day, He went out, and departed into a solitary place, and there prayed.

Him; and He laid His hands on every one of them, and healed them.

And devils also came out of many, crying out, and saying, Thou art Christ the Son of God. And He, rebuking *them*, suffered them not to speak: for they knew that He was Christ.

And in the morning, rising up a great while before day, He went out, and departed into a solitary place, and there prayed.

And Simon and they that were with him followed after Him.

And when they had found Him, they said unto Him, All *men* seek for thee.

And He said unto them, Let us go into the next towns, that I may preach there also: for therefore came I forth.

And Jesus went about all Galilee, teaching in their synagogues, and preaching the gospel of the kingdom, and healing all manner of sickness and all manner of disease among the people.

And His fame went throughout all Syria: and **they brought unto** Him all sick people that were taken with divers diseases and torments, and those which were possessed with devils, and those which were lunatics, and those that had the palsy; and He healed them.

And there followed Him great multitudes of people from Galilee, and *from* Decapolis, and *from* Jerusalem and *from* Judea, and *from* beyond Jordan.

CHAPTER IX.

HE CLEANSETH THE LEPER

AND there came a leper to Him, beseeching Him, and kneeling down to Him, and saying unto Him,

If thou wilt, thou canst make me clean.

And Jesus, moved with compassion, put forth *His* hand, and touched him, and said unto him, I will; be thou clean.

And as soon as He had spoken, immediately the leprosy departed from him, and he was cleansed.

And He straitly charged him, and forthwith sent him away;

And saith unto him, See thou say nothing to any man: but go thy way, shew thyself to the priest, and offer for thy cleansing those things which Moses commanded, for a testimony unto them.

But he went out, and began to publish *it* much, and to blaze abroad the matter, insomuch that Jesus could no more openly enter into the city, but was without in desert places: and they came to Him from every quarter.

And He withdrew Himself into the wilderness, and prayed.

HE CURETH THE PALSIED.

AND again He entered into Capernaum after *some* days; and it was noised that He was in the house.

And straightway many were gathered together, insomuch that there was no room to receive *them*, no, not so much as about the door: and He preached the word unto them.

And they come unto Him, bringing one sick of the palsy, which was borne of four.

And when they could not come nigh unto Him for the press, they uncovered the roof where He was: and when they had broken *it* up, they let down the bed

"I will; be thou clean."

"I say unto thee, Arise, and take up thy bed, and go thy way into thine house."

wherein the sick of the palsy lay.

When Jesus saw their faith, He said unto the sick of the palsy, Son, thy sins be forgiven thee.

But there were certain of the scribes sitting there, and reasoning in their hearts,

Why doth this *man* thus speak blasphemies? who can forgive sins but God only?

And immediately, when Jesus perceived in His spirit that they so reasoned within themselves, He said unto them, Why reason ye these things in your hearts?

Whether it is easier to say to the sick of the palsy, *Thy* sins be forgiven thee; or to say, Arise, and take up thy bed and walk?

But that ye may know that the Son of Man hath power on earth to forgive sins, (He saith to the sick of the palsy,)

I say unto thee, Arise, take up thy bed, and walk.

And immediately he arose, took up the bed, and went forth before them all; insomuch that they were all amazed, and glorified God, saying, We never saw it on this fashion.

HE TEACHETH OUT OF PETER'S SHIP.

AND it came to pass, that, as the people pressed upon Him to hear the word of God, He stood by the lake of Gennesaret.

And saw two ships standing by the lake; but the fishermen were gone out of them, and were washing *their* nets.

And He entered into one of the ships, which was Simon's, and prayed him that he would thrust out a little from the land. And

He sat down, and taught the people out of the ship.

Now when He had left speaking, He said unto Simon, Launch out into the deep, and let down your nets for a draught.

And Simon answering said unto Him, Master, we have toiled all the night, and have taken nothing: nevertheless at thy word I will let down the net.

And when they had this done, they inclosed a great multitude of fishes: and their net brake.

And they beckoned unto *their* partners, which were in the other ship, that they should come and help them. And they came, and filled both the ships, so that they began to sink.

When Simon Peter saw *it* he fell down at Jesus' knees, saying, Depart from me; for I am a sinful man, O Lord.

For he was astonished, and all that were with him, at the draught of the fishes which they had taken:

And so *was* also James, and John, the sons of Zebedee, which were partners with Simon. And Jesus said unto Simon, Fear not; from henceforth thou shalt catch men.

And when they had brought their ships to land, they forsook all, and followed Him.

¶ And after these things He went forth, and saw a publican, named Levi, sitting at the receipt of custom: and He said unto him, Follow me.

And he left all, rose up, and followed Him.

And Levi made Him a great feast in his own house: and there was a great company of publicans and of

"Follow Me."

"I came not to call the righteous, but sinners to repentance."

others that sat down with them.

But the scribes and Pharisees murmured against His disciples, saying, Why do you eat and drink with publicans and sinners?

And Jesus answering said unto them, They that are whole need not a physician; but they that are sick.

I came not to call the righteous, but sinners to repentance.

And they said unto Him, Why do the disciples of John fast often, and make prayers, and likewise *the disciples* of the Pharisees; but thine eat and drink?

And He said unto them, Can ye make the children of the bridechamber, fast while the bridegroom is with them?

But the days will come, when the bridegroom shall be taken away from them, and then shall they fast in those days.

And He spake also a parable unto them; No man putteth a piece of a new garment upon an old; if otherwise, then both the new maketh a rent, and the piece that was *taken* out of the new agreeth not with the old.

And no man putteth new wine into old bottles; else the new wine will burst the bottles, and be spilled, and the bottles shall perish.

But new wine must be put into new bottles; and both are preserved.

No man also having drunk old *wine* straightway desireth new; for he saith The old is better.

CHAPTER X.

BETHESDA.

AFTER this there was a feasts of the Jews; and Jesus went up to Jerusalem.

Now there is at Jerusalem by the sheep *market* a pool, which is called in the Hebrew tongue Bethesda, having five porches.

In these lay a great multitude of impotent folk, of blind, halt, withered, waiting for the moving of the water.

For an angel went down at a certain season into the pool, and troubled the water: whosoever then first after the troubling of the water stepped in was made whole of whatsoever disease he had.

And a certain man was there, which had an infirmity thirty and eight years.

When Jesus saw him lie, and knew that he had been now a long time *in that case*, He saith unto him, Wilt thou be made whole?

The impotent man answered Him, Sir, I have no man when the water is troubled, to put me into the pool: but while I am coming, another steppeth down before me.

Jesus saith unto him, Rise, take up thy bed, and walk.

And immediately the man was made whole, and took up his bed, and walked: and on the same day was the sabbath.

The Jews therefore said unto him that was cured, It is the sabbath day: it is not lawful for thee to carry *thy* bed.

He answered them, He that made me whole, the same said unto me, Take up thy bed, and walk.

Then asked they him, What man is that which said unto thee, Take up thy bed, and walk?

And he that was healed wist not who it was: for Jesus had conveyed Himself

Jesus saith unto him, Rise, take up thy bed, and walk.

away, a multitude being in *that* place.

Afterward Jesus findeth him in the temple, and said unto him, Behold, thou art made whole: sin no more, lest a worse thing come unto thee.

The man departed, and told the Jews that it was Jesus, which had made him whole.

And therefore did the Jews persecute Jesus, and sought to slay Him, because He had done these things on the sabbath day.

But Jesus answered them, My Father worketh hitherto, and I work.

Therefore the Jews sought the more to kill Him, because He not only had broken the sabbath, but said also that God was His Father, making himself equal with God.

Then answered Jesus and said unto them, Verily, verily, I say unto you, The Son can do nothing of Himself, but what He seeth the Father do: for what things soever He doeth, these also doeth the Son likewise.

For the Father loveth the Son, and sheweth Him all things that Himself doeth: and He will shew Him greater works than these, that ye may marvel.

For as the Father raiseth up the dead, and quickeneth *them;* even so the Son quickeneth whom He will.

For the Father judgeth no man, but hath committed all judgment unto the Son:

That all *men* should honour the Son, even as they honour the Father. He that honoureth not the Son honoureth not the Father which hath sent Him.

Verily, verily, I say unto you, He that heareth my word, and believeth on Him that sent me, hath everlasting life, and shall not come into condemnation: but is passed from death unto life.

Verily, verily, I say unto you, The hour is coming and now is, when the dead shall hear the voice of the Son of God: and they that hear shall live.

For as the Father hath life in Himself; so hath He given to the Son to have life in Himself;

And hath given Him authority to execute judgment also, because He is the Son of man.

Marvel not at this: for the hour is coming, in the which all that are in the graves shall hear His voice,

And shall come forth; they that have done good, unto the resurrection of life? and they that have done evil, unto the resursection of damnation.

I can of mine own self do nothing: as I hear, I judge: and my judgment is just; because I seek not my own will, but the will of the Father which hath sent me,

If I bear witness of myself, my witness is not true.

There is another that beareth witness of me; and I know that the witness which He witnesseth of me is true.

Ye sent unto John, and he bare witness unto the truth.

But I receive not testimony from man: but these things I say, that ye might be saved.

He was a burning and a shining light: and ye were willing for a season to rejoice in his light.

But I have greater witness than *that* of John: for the works which the Father hath given me to finish, the same works that I do, bear

"Search the Scriptures; for in them ye think ye have eternal life; and they are they which testify of Me."

witness of me, that the Father hath sent me.

And the Father Himself, which hath sent me, hath borne witness of me, ye have neither heard His voice at any time, nor seen His shape.

And ye have not His word abiding in you: for whom He hath sent, Him ye believe not.

¶ Search the Scriptures; for in them ye think ye have eternal life: and they are they which testify of me.

And ye will not come to me, that ye might have life.

I receive not honour from men.

But I know you, that ye have not the love of God in you.

I am come in my Father's name, and ye received me not: if another shall come in his own name, him ye will receive.

How can ye believe, which receive honour one of another, and seek not the honour that *cometh* from God only?

Do not think that I will accuse you to the Father: there is *one* that accuseth you, *even* Moses, in whom ye trust.

For had ye believed Moses, ye would have believed me: for he wrote of me.

But if ye believe not his writings, how shall ye believe my words?

CHAPTER XI.

THE SON OF MAN LORD EVEN OF THE SABBATH.

AND it came to pass, that He went through the corn fields on the sabbath day; and His disciples were an hungered, and began to pluck the ears of corn, as they went, and to eat, rubbing *them* in *their* hands.

But when the Pharisees saw *it*, they said unto Him, Behold, thy disciples do that which is not lawful to do upon the Sabbath day; Why do they on the sabbath day that which is not lawful?

And Jesus answering them said, Have ye not read so much as this, what David did, when he had need, and was an hungered, he, and they that were with him?

How he went into the house of God in the days of Abiathar the high priest, and did eat the shew bread, which was not lawful for him to eat, neither for them which were with him, but only for the priests, and gave also to them which were with him?

Or have ye not read in the law, how that on the sabbath days the priests in the temple profane the sabbath, and are blameless?

But I say unto you, That in this place is *one* greater than the temple.

But if ye had known what this meaneth, "I will have mercy, and not sacrifice," ye would not have condemned the guiltless.

And He said unto them, The sabbath was made for man, and not man for the sabbath: and therefore the Son of man is Lord also of the sabbath day.

And when He was departed thence, He went into their synagogue, and taught: and there was a man there whose right hand was withered.

And the scribes and Pharisees watched Him, whether He would heal him on the sabbath day; (that they

"The sabbath was made for man, and not man for the sabbath."

might find an accusation against Him).

And they asked Him, saying, Is it lawful to heal on the sabbath days?

But He knew their thoughts, and said to the man which had the withered hand, Rise up and stand forth in the midst. And he arose and stood forth.

Then said Jesus unto them, I will ask you one thing: Is it lawful on the sabbath days to do good, or to do evil? to save life, or to destroy *it*? but they held their peace.

And looking round about upon them all, He said unto them, What man shall there be among you, that shall have one sheep, and if it fall into a pit on the sabbath day, will he not lay hold on it, and lift *it* out?

How much then is a man better than a sheep? Wherefore it is lawful to do well on the sabbath days.

And when He had looked round about on them with anger, being grieved for the hardness of their hearts,

Then saith He to the man, Stretch forth thine hand. And he stretched *it* forth; and it was restored whole, like as the other.

And the Pharisees were filled with madness; and went forth and communed one with another what they might do to Jesus; and straightway took counsel with the Herodians how they might destroy Him.

But Jesus withdrew himself with His disciples to the sea: and a great multitude from Galilee followed Him, and from Judea,

And from Jerusalem, and from Idumea, and *from* beyond Jordan; and they about Tyre and Sidon, a great multitude, when they had heard what great things He did, came unto Him.

And He spake to His disciples, that a small ship should wait on Him because of the multitude, lest they should throng Him.

For He had healed many; insomuch that they pressed upon Him for to touch Him, as many as had plagues.

And unclean spirits, when they saw Him, fell down before Him, and cried, saying, Thou art the Son of God.

And He straitly charged them that they should not make Him known.

That it might be fulfilled which was spoken by Esaias the prophet, saying,

Behold My servant, whom I have chosen; my Beloved, in whom my soul is well pleased: I will put my Spirit upon Him, and He shall shew judgment to the Gentiles.

He shall not strive, nor cry; neither shall any man hear His voice in the streets.

A bruised reed shall He not break, and smoking flax shall He not quench, till He send forth judgment unto victory.

And in His name shall the Gentiles trust.

¶ And it came to pass in those days, that Jesus went out into a mountain to pray, and continued all night in prayer to God.

And when it was day, He called *unto Him* his disciples: and of them He chose twelve, whom also He named apostles; that they should be with Him, and that He might send them forth to preach.

And to have power to

The Pharisees counsel with the Herodians how they might destroy Him.

heal sicknesses, and to cast out devils.

Simon, (whom He also named Peter,) and Andrew his brother, James and John, Philip and Bartholomew,

Matthew and Thomas, James the *son* of Alpheus, and Simon called Zelotes,

And Judas *the brother* of James, and Judas Iscariot, which also was the traitor.

And He came down with them, and stood in the plain, and the company of His disciples, and a great multitude of people out of all Judea and Jerusalem, and from the sea coast of Tyre and Sidon, which came to hear Him, and to be healed of their diseases;

And they that were vexed with unclean spirits: and they were healed.

THE SERMON ON THE MOUNT.

And seeing the multitudes, He went up into a mountain: and when He was set, his disciple came unto Him:

And He opened His mouth, and taught them, saying,

Blessed *are* the poor in spirit: for theirs is the kingdom of heaven.

Blessed *are* they that mourn: for they shall be comforted.

Blessed *are* the meek: for they shall inherit the earth.

Blessed *are* they which do hunger and thirst after righteousness: for they shall be filled.

Blessed *are* the merciful: for they shall obtain mercy.

Blessed *are* the pure in heart: for they shall see God.

Blessed *are* the peacemakers: for they shall be called the children of God.

Blessed *are* they which are persecuted for righteousness' sake : for theirs is the kingdom of heaven.

Blessed are ye when *men* shall revile you, and persecute *you*, and shall say all manner of evil against you falsely for my sake.

Rejoice ye in that day, and leap for joy : for behold, your reward *is* great in heaven : for in the like manner did their fathers unto the prophets.

But woe unto you that are rich ! for ye have received your consolation.

Woe unto you that are full ! for ye shall hunger. Woe unto you that laugh now ! for ye shall mourn and weep.

Woe unto you when all men shall speak well of you ! for so did their fathers to the false prophets.

¶ Ye are the salt of the earth : but if the salt has lost its savour, wherewith shall it be salted ? it is thenceforth good for nothing, but to be cast out, and to be trodden under foot of men.

Ye are the light of the world. A city that is set upon a hill cannot be hid.

Neither do men light a candle, and put it under a bushel, but on a candlestick ; and it giveth light unto all that are in the house.

Let your light so shine before men, that they may see your good works, and glorify your Father which is in heaven.

Think not that I am come to destroy the law, or the prophets ; I am not come to destroy, but to fulfil.

For verily I say unto you, Till heaven and earth pass, one jot or one tittle shall in no wise pass from the law, till all be fulfilled.

Whosoever therefore shall

"Blessed are the poor in spirit: for theirs is the kingdom of heaven."

break one of these least commandments, and shall teach men so, he shall be called the least in the kingdom of heaven: but whosoever shall do and teach *them*, the same shall be called great in the kingdom of heaven.

For I say unto you, That except your rightousness shall exceed *the rightousness* of the scribes and Pharisees, ye shall in no case enter into the kingdom of heaven.

Ye have heard that it was said by them of old time, Thou shalt not kill; and whosoever shall kill shall be in danger of the judgment;

But I say unto you, That whosoever is angry with his brother without a cause shall be in danger of the judgment; and whosoever shall say to his brother, Raca, shall be in danger of the council; but whosoever shall say, Thou fool, shall be in danger of hell fire.

Therefore if thou bring thy gift to the altar, and there rememberest that thy brother hath aught against thee;

Leave there thy gift before the altar, and go thy way; first be reconciled to thy brother, and then come and offer thy gift.

Agree with thine adversary quickly, while thou art in the way with him; lest at any time the adversary deliver thee to the judge, and the judge deliver thee to the officer, and thou be cast into prison.

Verily, I say unto thee, Thou shalt by no means come out thence, till thou hast paid the uttermost farthing.

Ye have heard that it was said by them of old time, Thou shalt not commit adultery:

But I say unto you, That whosoever looketh on a woman to lust after her hath committed adultery with her already in his heart.

And if thy right eye offend thee, pluck it out, and cast *it* from thee; for it is profitable for thee that one of thy members should perish, and not *that* thy whole body should be cast into hell.

And if thy right hand offend thee, cut it off, and cast *it* from thee: for it is profitable for thee that one of thy members should perish, and not *that* thy whole body should be cast into hell.

It hath been said, Whosoever shall put away his wife, let him give her a writing of divorcement:

But I say unto you, That whosoever shall put his wife away saving for the cause of fornication, causeth her to commit adultery: and whosoever shall marry her that is divorced committeth adultery.

Again, ye have heard that it hath been said by them of old time, Thou shalt not forswear thyself, but shalt perform unto the Lord thine oaths:

But I say unto you, Swear not at all; neither by heaven; for it is God's throne:

Nor by the earth; for it is his footstool: neither by Jerusalem; for it is the city of the great King.

Neither shalt thou swear by thy head, because thou canst not make one hair white or black.

But let your communication be, Yea, yea; Nay, nay: for whatsoever is more than these cometh of evil.

Ye have heard that it hath been said, An eye for

an eye, and a tooth for a tooth:

But I say unto you, That ye resist not evil: but whosoever shall smite thee on thy right cheek, turn to him the other also.

And if any man will sue thee at the law, and take away thy coat, let him have *thy* cloak also.

And whosoever shall compel thee to go a mile, go with him twain.

Give to every man that asketh of thee, and from him that would borrow of thee turn not thou away; and of him that taketh away thy goods ask *them* not again.

And as ye would that men should do to you, do ye also to them likewise.

Ye have heard that it hath been said, Thou shalt love thy neighbour, and hate thine enemy.

But I say unto you, Love your enemies, bless them that curse you, do good to them that hate you, and pray for them which despitefully use you, and persecute you;

That you may be the children of your Father which is in heaven: for he maketh his sun to rise on the evil and on the good, and sendeth rain on the just and on the unjust.

For if ye love them which love you, what reward have ye? do not even the publicans the same?

And if ye salute your brethren only, what do ye more *than others?* do not even the publicans so?

And if ye do good to them which do good to you, what thank have ye? for sinners also do even the same.

And if ye lend *to them* of whom ye hope to receive, what thank have ye? for sinners also lend to sinners, to receive as much again.

But love ye your enemies, and do good, and lend, hoping for nothing again; and your reward shall be great, and ye shall be the children of the Highest: for He is kind unto the unthankful and *to* the evil.

Be ye merciful, as your Father also is merciful.

Be ye therefore perfect even as your Father which is in heaven is perfect.

CHAPTER XII.

TAKE heed that ye do not your alms before men, to be seen of them: otherwise ye have no reward of your Father which is in heaven.

Therefore when thou doest *thine* alms, do not sound a trumpet before thee as the hypocrites do in the synagogues and in the streets, that they may have glory of men. Verily I say unto you, They have their reward.

But when thou doest alms, let not thy left hand know what thy right hand doeth:

That thine alms may be in secret: and thy Father which seeth in secret, Himself shall reward thee openly.

And when thou prayest, thou shalt not be as the hypocrits *are:* for they love to pray standing in the synagogues and in the corners of the streets, that they may be seen of men. Verily I say unto you, They have their reward.

But thou, when thou prayest, enter into thy closet, and when thou hast shut thy door, pray to thy Father which is in secret; and thy Father which seeth in secret shall reward thee openly.

But when ye pray, use

not vain repetitions, as the heathen *do:* for they think that they shall be heard for their much speaking.

Be ye not therefore like unto them: for your Father knoweth what things ye have need of, before ye ask Him.

After this manner therefore pray ye: Our Father who art in Heaven, Hallowed be Thy name.

Thy kingdom come, Thy will be done in earth, *as it is* in heaven.

Give us this day our daily bread.

And forgive us our debts as we forgive our debtors.

And lead us not into temptation, but deliver us from evil: for Thine is the kingdom, and the power, and the glory, forever. Amen.

For if ye forgive men their trespasses, your heavenly Father will also forgive you:

But if ye forgive not men their trespasses, neither will your Father forgive your trespasses.

Moreover when ye fast, be not, as the hypocrites, of a sad countenance: for they disfigure their faces, that they may appear unto men to fast. Verily I say unto you, They have their reward.

But thou, when thou fastest, anoint thine head, and wash thy face;

That thou appear not unto men to fast, but unto thy Father which is in secret: and thy Father which seeth in secret shall reward thee openly.

Lay not up for yourselves treasures upon earth, where moth and rust doth corrupt and where thieves break through and steal:

But lay up for yourselves

treasures in heaven, where neither moth nor rust doth corrupt, and where thieves do not break through nor steal:

For where your treasure is, there will your heart be also.

The light of the body is the eye: if therefore thine eye be single, thy whole body shall be full of light.

But if thine eye be evil, thy whole body shall be full of darkness. If therefore the light that is in thee be darkness, h o w great *is* that darkness!

¶ No man can serve two masters: for either he will hate the one, and love the other; or else he will hold to the one, and despise the other. Ye cannot serve God and mammon.

Therefore I say unto you, Take no thought for your life, what ye shall eat, or what ye shall drink; nor yet for your body, what ye shall put on. Is not the life more than meat, and the body than raiment?

Behold the fowls of the air: for they sow n o t, neither do they reap, nor gather into barns; yet your heavenly Father f e e d e t h them. Are ye not much better than they?

Which of you by taking thought can add one cubit unto his stature?

And why take ye thought for raiment? Consider the lilies of the field, how they grow; they toil not, neither do they spin:

And yet I say unto you, That even Solomon in all his glory was not arrayed like one of these.

Wherefore, if God so clothe the grass of the field, which to day is, and tomorrow is cast into the oven, *shall he* not much more *clothe* you, O ye of little faith?

Therefore take no thought, saying, What shall we eat? or, What shall we drink? or, Wherewithal shall we be clothed?

(For after all these things do the Gentiles seek:) for your heavenly Father knoweth that ye have need of all these things.

But seek ye first the kingdom of God, and His righteousness; and all these things shall be added unto you.

Take therefore no thought for the morrow: for the morrow shall take thought for the things of itself. Sufficient unto the day *is* the evil thereof.

¶ Judge not, that ye be not judged.

For with what judgment ye judge, ye shall be judged: and with what measure ye mete, it shall be measured to you again.

And why beholdest thou the mote that is in thy brother's eye, but considerest not the beam that is in thine own eye?

Or how wilt thou say to thy brother, Let me pull out the mote out of thine eye; and, behold, a beam *is* in thine own eye?

Thou hypocrite, first cast out the beam out of thine own eye; and then shalt thou see clearly to cast out the mote out of thy brother's eye.

Give not that which is holy unto the dogs, neither cast ye your pearls before swine, lest they trample them under their feet, and turn again and rend you.

Ask, and it shall be given you; seek, and ye shall find; knock, and it shall be opened unto you:

For every one that asketh

receiveth; and he that seeketh findeth; and to him that knocketh it shall be opened.

Or what man is there of you, whom if his son ask bread, will he give him a stone?

Or if he ask a fish, will he give him a serpent?

If ye then, being evil, know how to give good gifts unto your children, how much more shall your Father which is in heaven give good things to them that ask him?

Therefore all things whatsoever ye would that men should do to you, do ye even so to them: for this is the law and the prophets.

Enter ye in at the strait gate: for wide *is* the gate, and broad *is* the way, that leadeth to destruction, and many there be which go in thereat:

Because strait *is* the gate, and narrow *is* the way, which leadeth unto life, and few there be that find it.

Beware of false prophets, which come to you in sheep's clothing, but inwardly they are ravening wolves.

Ye shall know them by their fruits; for every tree is known by his own fruit. Of thorns men do not gather figs, nor of a bramble bush gather they grapes.

Even so every good tree bringeth forth good fruit; but a corrupt tree bringeth forth evil fruit.

A good tree cannot bring forth evil fruit, neither *can* a corrupt tree bring forth good fruit.

A good man out of the good treasure of his heart bringeth forth that which is good; and an evil man out of the evil treasure of his heart bringeth forth that which is evil: for of the abundance of the heart his mouth speaketh.

Wherefore by their fruits ye shall know them.

Every tree that bringeth not forth good fruit is hewn down, and cast into the fire.

And why call ye me, Lord, Lord, and do not the things which I say?

Not every one that saith unto me, Lord, Lord, shall enter into the kingdom of heaven; but he that doeth the will of my Father which is in heaven.

Many will say to me in that day, Lord, Lord, have we not prophesied in thy name? and in Thy name have cast out devils? and in thy name done many wonderful works?

And then will I profess unto them, I never knew you: depart from me, ye that work iniquity.

Therefore whosoever heareth these sayings of mine, and doeth them, I will liken him unto a wise man, which built his house upon a rock:

And the rain descended, and the floods came, and the winds blew, and beat upon that house: and it fell not: for it was founded upon a rock.

And every one that heareth these sayings of mine, and doeth them not, shall be likened unto a foolish man, which built his house upon the sand:

And the rain descended, and the floods came, and the winds blew, and beat upon that house; and it fell: and great was the fall of it.

And it came to pass, when Jesus had ended these sayings, the people were astonished at His doctrine:

For He taught them as *one* having authority, and not as the scribes.

CHAPTER XIII.

HEALETH THE CENTURION'S SERVANT

NOW when He had ended all His sayings in the audience of the people, He entered into Capernaum.

And a certain centurion's servant, who was dear unto him, was sick, and ready to die.

And when he heard of Jesus, He sent unto Him the elders of the Jews, beseeching Him that He would come and heal his servant.

And when they came to Jesus, they besought Him instantly, saying, That he was worthy for whom He should do this:

For he loveth our nation, and he hath built us a synagogue.

Then Jesus went with them. And when He was now not far from the house, the centurion sent friends to Him, saying unto Him, Lord, trouble not thyself; for I am not worthy that thou shouldest enter under my roof:

Wherefore neither thought I myself worthy to come unto thee: but say in a word, and my servant shall be healed.

For I also am a man set under authority, having under me soldiers, and I say unto one, Go, and he goeth; and to another, Come, and he cometh; and to my servant, Do this, and he doeth it.

When Jesus heard these things, He marvelled, and turned Him about, and said unto the people that followed Him, I say unto you, I have not found so great faith, no, not in Israel.

"I say unto you, I have not found so great faith; no, not in Israel."

And I say unto you, That many shall come from the east and west, and shall sit down with Abraham, and Isaac, and Jacob, in the kingdom of heaven:

But the children of the kingdom shall be cast out into outer darkness; there shall be weeping and gnashing of teeth.

And they that were sent, returning to the house, found the servant whole that had been sick.

RAISETH FROM DEATH THE WIDOW'S SON.

¶ AND it came to pass the day after, that He went into a city called Nain; and many of His disciples went with Him, and much people.

Now when He came nigh to the gate of the city behold, there was a dead man carried out; the only son of his mother, and she was a widow; and much people of the city was with her.

And when the Lord saw her, He had compassion on her, and said unto her, Weep not.

And He came and touched the bier; and they that bare *him* stood still. And He said, Young man, I say unto thee, Arise.

And he that was dead sat up, and began to speak. And He delivered him to his mother.

And there came a fear on all; and they glorified God, saying, That a great prophet is risen up among us; and, that God hath visited His people.

And this rumor of Him went forth throughout all Judea, and throughout all the region round about.

And the disciples of John shewed him of all these things. And when John had heard of the works of

Christ, he, calling *unto him* in the prison two of his disciples, sent *them* to Jesus, saying, Art thou He that should come? or look we for another!

When the men were come unto Him, they said, John Baptist hath sent us unto thee saying, Art thou He that should come? or look we for another?

And in that same hour He cured many of *their* infirmities and plagues, and of evil spirits; and unto many *that were* blind He gave sight.

Then Jesus answering said unto them, Go your way, and tell John what things ye have seen and heard; how that the blind see, the lame walk, the lepers are cleansed, the deaf hear, the dead are raised, to the poor the gospel is preached.

And blessed is *he*, whosoever shall not be offended in me.

And when the messengers of John were departed He began to speak unto the people concerning John, What went ye into the wilderness for to see? A reed shaken with the wind?

But what went ye out for to see? A man clothed in soft raiment? Behold, they which are gorgeously apparelled, and live delicately, are in king's courts.

But what went ye out for to see? A prophet? Yea, I say unto you, and much more than a prophet.

This is *he*, of whom it is written, Behold, I send my messenger before thy face, which shall prepare thy way before thee.

For I say unto you, Among those that are born of women there is not a greater prophet than John the Baptist: but he that is

AND HE DELIVERED HIM TO HIS MOTHER.

least in the kingdom of God is greater than he.

And from the days of John the Baptist until now the kingdom of heaven suffereth violence, and the violent take it by force.

For all the prophets and the law prophesied until John.

And if ye will receive *it*, this is Elias, which was for to come.

He that hath ears to hear, let him hear.

And all the people that heard *Him*, and the publicans, justified God, being baptized with the baptism of John:

But the Pharisees and lawyers rejected the counsel of God against themselves, being not baptized of him.

And the Lord said, whereunto then shall I liken the men of this generation? and to what are they like?

They are like unto children sitting in the marketplace, and calling one to another, saying, We have piped unto you, and ye have not danced; we have mourned to you. and ye have not wept.

For John the Baptist came neither eating bread nor drinking wine; and ye say, He hath a devil.

The Son of Man is come eating and drinking; and ye say, Behold a gluttonous man, and a winebibber, a friend of publicans and sinners!

But wisdom is justified of all her children.

Then began He to upbraid the cities wherein most of His mighty works were done, because they repented not:

Woe, unto thee, Chorazin! woe unto thee, Bethsaida! for if the mighty works, which were done in you, had been done in Tyre and Sidon, they would have repented long ago in sackcloth and ashes.

But I say unto you, it will be more tolerable for Tyre and Sidon at the day of judgment, than for you.

And thou Capernaum, which art exalted unto heaven, shall be brought down to hell; for if the mighty works, which have been done in thee, had been done in Sodom, it would have remained until this day.

But I say unto you, That it shall be more tolerable for the land of Sodom in the day of judgment, than for thee.

¶ At that time Jesus answered and said, I thank thee, O Father, Lord of heaven and earth, because thou hast hid these things from the wise and prudent, and hast revealed them unto babes.

Even so, Father; for so it seemed good in thy sight.

All things are delivered unto me of my Father: and no man knoweth the Son, but the Father; neither knoweth any man the Father, save the Son, and *he* to whomsoever the Son will reveal *Him*.

Come unto me, all *ye* that labour and are heavy laden, and I will give you rest.

Take my yoke upon you, and learn of me: for I am meek and lowly of heart; and ye shall find rest unto your souls.

For my yoke *is* easy, and my burden is light.

CHAPTER XIV.

JESUS, SIMON'S GUEST,

AND one of the Pharisees desired Him that he would eat with him.

To whomsoever much is forgiven, the same loveth much.

And He went into the Pharisee's house, and sat down to meat.

And, behold, a woman in the city, which was a sinner, when she knew that *Jesus* sat at meat in the Pharisee's house, brought an alabaster box of ointment,

And stood at His feet behind *Him* weeping, and began to wash His feet with tears, and did wipe *them* with the hairs of her head, and kissed His feet, and anointed *them* with the ointment.

Now when the Pharisee which had bidden Him saw *it*, he spake within himself, saying, This man, if He were a prophet, would have known who and what manner of woman *this is* that toucheth Him: for she is a sinner.

And Jesus answering said unto him, Simon, I have somewhat to say unto thee. And he saith, Master, say on.

There was a certain creditor which had two debtors; the one owed five hundred pence, and the other, fifty.

And when they had nothing to pay, he frankly forgave them both. Tell me therefore, which of them will love him most?

Simon answered and said, I suppose that *he*, to whom he forgave most. And He said unto him, Thou hast rightly judged.

And He turned to the woman, and said unto Simon, Seest thou this woman? I entered into thine house; thou gavest me no water for my feet; but she hath washed my feet with tears, and wiped *them* with the hairs of her head.

Thou gavest me no kiss: but this woman, since the

time I came in, hath not ceased to kiss my feet.

My head with oil thou didst not anoint but this woman hath anointed my feet with ointment.

Wherefore I say unto thee, Her sins, which are many, are forgiven; for she loveth much: but to whom little is forgiven, *the same* loveth little.

And He said unto her, Thy sins are forgiven.

And they that sat at meat with Him began to say within themselves, Who is this that forgiveth sins also?

And He said to the woman, Thy faith has saved thee: go in peace.

And it came to pass afterward, that He went throughout every city and village, preaching and shewing the glad tidings of the kingdom of God: and the twelve *were* with Him.

And certain women, which had been healed of evil spirits and infirmities, Mary called Magdalene, out of whom went seven devils,

And Joanna the wife of Chuza, Herod's steward, and Susanna, and many others, which ministered unto Him of their substance; and they went into a house.

And the multitude cometh together again, so that they could not so much as eat bread.

And when His friends heard *of it*, they went out to lay hold on Him: for they said, He is beside Himself.

¶ Then was brought unto Him one possessed with a devil, blind, and dumb: and He healed him, insomuch that the blind and dumb both spake and saw.

And all the people were

Mary called Magdalene.

amazed, and said, Is not this the Son of David?

But when the Pharisees, and the scribes which came down from Jerusalem heard *it*, they said, He hath Beelzebub: and, This *fellow* doth not cast out devils, but by Beelzebub, the prince of the devils.

But Jesus knew their thoughts; and He then called them *unto Him*, and said unto them in parables, How can Satan cast out Satan?

Every kingdom divided against itself is brought to desolation, and cannot stand: and every city or house divided against itself shall not stand:

And if Satan rise up against himself, and cast out Satan, he is divided against himself; how shall then his kingdom stand?

And if I by Beelzebub cast out devils, by whom do your children cast *them* out? therefore they shall be your judges.

But if I cast out devils by the spirit of God then the kingdom of God is come unto you.

Or else, how can one enter into a strong man's house, and spoil his goods, except he first bind the strong man?

When a strong man armed keepeth his palace, his goods are in peace: but when a stronger than he shall come upon him, and overcome him, he taketh from him all armour wherein he trusted, and divideth his spoils.

He that is not with me is against me; and he that gathereth not with me scattereth abroad.

Verily, I say unto you, All manner of sins shall be forgiven unto the sons of men, and blasphemies wherewith soever they shall blaspheme: but the blasphemy *against* the *Holy* Ghost shall not be forgiven unto men.

And whosoever speaketh a word against the Son of Man, it shall be forgiven him: but whosoever speaketh against the Holy Ghost, it shall not be forgiven him, neither in this world, neither in the *world* to come;

He that shall blaspheme against the Holy Ghost hath never forgiveness, but is in danger of eternal damnation.

(Because they said, He hath an unclean spirit).

Either make the tree good, and his fruit good; or else make the tree corrupt, or his fruit corrupt: for the tree is known by *his* fruit.

O generation of vipers, how can ye, being evil, speak good things? for out of the abundance of the heart the mouth speaketh.

A good man out of the good treasure of the heart bringeth forth good things: and an evil man out of the evil treasure bringeth forth evil things.

But I say unto you, That every idle word that men shall speak, they shall give account thereof in the day of judgment.

For by thy words thou shalt be justified, and by thy words thou shalt be condemned.

¶ Then certain of the scribes and of the Pharisees answered, saying, Master, we would see a sign from thee.

But He answered and said unto them, An evil and adulterous generation seeketh after a sign; and there shall no sign be given to it, but the sign of the prophet Jonas;

For as Jonas was three

days and three nights in the whale's belly; so shall the Son of Man be three days and three nights in the heart of the earth.

The men of Ninevah shall rise in judgment with this generation, and shall condemn it: because they repented at the preaching of Jonas; and, behold, a greater than Jonas *is* here.

The queen of the south shall rise up in the judgment with this generation, and shall condemn it: for she came from the uttermost parts of the earth to hear the wisdom of Solomon; and, behold, a greater than Solomon *is* here.

No man, when he hath lighted a candle, covereth it with a vessel, or putteth *it* under a bed; but setteth *it* on a candlestick, that they which enter in may see the light.

The light of the body is the eye: therefore when thine eye is single, thy whole body also is full of light; but when *thine eye* is evil, thy body also *is* full of darkness.

Take heed therefore, that the light which is in thee be not darkness.

If thy whole body therefore *be* full of light, having no part dark, the whole shall be full of light, as when the bright shining of a candle doth give thee light.

When the unclean spirit is gone out of a man, he walketh through dry places, seeking rest; and finding none, he saith, I will return unto my house whence I came out.

And when he cometh, he findeth *it* swept and garnished.

Then goeth he and taketh with himself seven other

spirits more wicked than himself, and they enter in and dwell there: and the last *state* of that man is worse than the first; Even so shall it be also unto this wicked generation.

And it came to pass, as He spake these things, a certain woman of the company lifted up her voice, and said unto Him, Blessed *is* the womb that bare thee, and the paps which thou hast sucked!

But He said, Yea, rather blessed *are* they that hear the word of God and keep it.

While He yet talked to the people, behold, *His* mother and His brethren stood without, desiring to speak with Him, and could not come at Him for the press; and, standing without, sent unto Him, calling Him.

And the multitude sat about Him, and one said unto Him, Behold thy mother and thy brethren without seek for thee, desiring to speak with thee.

But He answered and said unto him that told Him, Who is my mother? and who are my brethren?

And He stretched forth His hand toward His disciples, and said, Behold my mother and my brethren!

For whosoever shall do the will of my Father which is in heaven, the same is my brother, and sister, and mother.

My mother and my brethren are these which hear the word of God, and do it.

CHAPTER XV.

AND as He spake a certain Pharisee besought Him to dine with him; and

He went in, and sat down to meat.

And when the Pharisee saw *it*, he marvelled that He had not first washed before dinner.

And the Lord said unto him, Now do ye Pharisees make clean the outside of the cup and the platter; but your inward part is full of ravening and wickedness.

Ye fools! did not He that made that which is without, make that which is within also?

But rather give alms of such things as ye have; and, behold, all things are clean unto you.

But woe unto you Pharisees! for ye tithe mint and rue and all manner of herbs, and pass over judgment and the love of God: these ought ye to have done, and not to leave the other undone.

Woe unto you, Pharisees! for ye love the uppermost seats in the synagogues and greetings in the markets.

Woe unto you, scribes and Pharisees, hypocrites! for ye are as graves which appear not, and the men that walk over *them* are not aware *of them*.

Then answered one of the lawyers, and said unto Him, Master, thus saying, thou reproachest us also.

And He said, Woe unto you also, *ye* lawyers! for ye lade men with burdens grievous to be borne, and ye yourselves touch not the burdens with one of your fingers.

Woe unto you! for ye build the sepulchres of the prophets, and your fathers killed them.

Truly ye bear witness that ye allow the deeds of your fathers: for they indeed killed them, and ye build their sepulchres.

Therefore also said the wisdom of God, I will send them prophets and apostles, and *some* of them they shall slay and persecute :

That the blood of all the prophets, which was shed from the foundation of the world, may be required of this generation ;

From the blood of Abel unto the blood of Zacharias, which perished between the altar and the temple : verily I say unto you, It shall be required of this generation.

Woe unto you, lawyers! for ye have taken away the key of knowledge: ye entered not in yourselves, and them that were entering in ye hindered.

And as He said these things unto them, the scribes and the Pharisees began to urge *Him* vehemently, and to provoke Him to speak of many things.

Laying wait for Him, and seeking to catch something out of His mouth, that they might accuse Him.

In the mean time when there were gathered together an innumerable multitude of people, insomuch that they trode one upon another, He began to say unto His disciples first of all, Beware ye of the leaven of the Pharisees, which is hypocrisy.

For there is nothing covered, that shall not be revealed : neither hid, that shall not be known.

Therefore, whatsoever ye have spoken in darkness shall be heard in the light ; and that which ye have spoken in the ear in closets shall be proclaimed upon the housetops.

And I say unto you, my friends, Be not afraid of

them that kill the body, and after that have no more that they can do.

But I will forewarn you whom ye shall fear, Fear Him, which after He hath killed hath power to cast into hell; yea, I say unto you, Fear Him!

Are not five sparrows sold for two farthings? and not one of them is forgotten before God.

But even the very hairs of your head are all numbered. Fear not therefore: ye are of more value than many sparrows.

Also I say unto you, Whosoever shall confess me before men, him shall the Son of Man also confess before the angels of God.

But he that denieth me before men shall be denied before the angels of God.

And when they bring you unto the synagogues, and *unto* magistrates, and powers, take ye no thought how or what thing ye shall answer, or what ye shall say: for the Holy Ghost shall teach you in the same hour what ye ought to say.

¶ And one of the company said unto Him, Master speak to my brother, that he divide the inheritance with me.

And He said unto him, Man, who made me a judge or a divider over you?

And He said unto them, Take heed, and beware of covetousness: for a man's life consisteth not in the abundance of the things which he possesseth.

And He spake a parable unto them, saying, The ground of a certain rich man brought forth plentifully:

And he thought within himself, saying, What shall I do, because I have no room where to bestow my fruits?

And he said, This will I do: I will pull down my barns, and build greater; and there will I bestow all my f r u i t s and my goods.

And I will say to my soul, Soul, thou hast much goods laid up for many years; take thine ease, eat, drink, *and* be merry.

But God said unto him, *thou* fool, this night thy soul shall be required of thee: then whose shall those things be, which thou hast provided?

So *is* he that layeth up treasure for himself, and is not rich toward God.

And He said unto His disciples, Therefore I say unto you, Take no thought for your life, what ye shall eat; neither for the body, what ye shall put on.

The life is more than meat, and the body *is more* than raiment.

Consider the ravens: for they neither sow nor reap; which neither have storehouse nor barn; and God feedeth them: how much more are ye better than the fowls?

And which of you with taking thought can add to his stature one cubit?

If ye then be not able to do that thing which is least, why take ye thought for the rest?

Consider the lilies how they grow: they toil not, they spin not; and yet I say unto you, that Solomon in all his glory was not arrayed like one of these.

If then God so clothe the grass, which is to-day in the field, and to-morrow is cast in to the oven; how much more *will He clothe* you, O ye of little faifh?

And seek not ye what ye

"They toil not, neither do they spin."

shall eat, or what ye shall drink, neither be ye of doubtful mind.

For all these things do the nations of the world seek after : and your Father knoweth that ye have need of these things.

But rather seek ye the kingdom of God; and all these things shall be added unto you.

Fear not, little flock; for it is your Father's good pleasure to give you the kingdom.

Sell that ye have, and give alms; provide yourselves bags which wax not old, a treasure in the heavens that failest not, where no thief approacheth, neither moth corrupteth.

For where your treasure is, there will your heart be also.

Let your loins be girded about, and *your* lights burning; and ye yourselves like unto men that wait for their lord, when he will return from the wedding; that when he cometh and knocketh, they may open unto him immediately.

Blessed *are* those servants, whom the lord when he cometh shall find watching! verily I say unto you, That he shall gird himself, and make them to sit down to meat, and will come forth and serve them.

And if he shall come in the second watch, or come in the third watch, and find *them* so, blessed are those servants!

And this know, that if the goodman of the house had known what hour the thief would come, he would have watched, and not have suffered his house to be broken through.

Be ye therefore ready also; for the Son of Man

cometh at an hour when ye think not.

Then Peter said unto Him, Lord, speakest thou this parable unto us, or even to all?

And the Lord said, Who then is that faithful and wise steward, whom *his* lord shall make ruler over his household, to give *them their* portion of meat in due season?

Blessed *is* that servant, whom his lord when he cometh shall find so doing!

Of a truth I say unto you, that he will make him ruler over all that he hath.

But and if that servant say in his heart, my lord delayeth his coming; and shall begin to beat the menservants and maidens, and to eat and drink, and to be drunken;

The lord of that servant will come in a day when he looketh not for *him*, and at an hour when he is not aware, and will cut him in sunder, and will appoint him his portion with the unbelievers.

And that servant, which knew his lord's will, and prepared not *himself*, neither did according to his will, shall be beaten with many *stripes*.

But he that knew not, and did commit things worthy of stripes shall be beaten with few *stripes*. For unto whomsoever much is given, of him shall be much required: and to whom men have committed much, of him they will ask the more.

I am come to send fire on the earth; and what will I, if it be already kindled?

But I have a baptism to be baptized with; and how am I straitened till it be accomplished!

Suppose ye that I am come to give peace on earth?

I tell you, Nay: but rather division: for from henceforth there shall be five in one house divided, three against two, and two against three.

The father shall be divided against the son, and the son against the father; the mother against the daughter, and the daughter against the mother; the mother-in-law against her daughter-in-law, and the daughter-in-law against her mother-in-law.

And He said also to the people, When ye see a cloud rise out of the west, straightway ye say, There cometh a shower; and so it is.

And when *ye see* the south wind blow, ye say, There will be heat; and it cometh to pass.

Ye hypocrites, ye can discern the face of the sky and of the earth; but how is it that ye do not discern this time?

Yea, and why even of yourselves judge ye not what is right?

When thou goest with thine adversary to the magistrate, *as thou art* in the way, give diligence that thou mayest be delivered from him; lest he hale thee to the judge, and the judge deliver thee to the officer, and the officer cast thee into prison.

I tell thee, thou shalt not depart thence, till thou hast paid the very last mite.

There were present at that season some that told Him of the Galileans, whose blood Pilate had mingled with their sacrifices.

And Jesus answering said unto them, Suppose ye that these Galileans were sinners above all the Galileans, because they suffered such things?

I tell you, Nay : but, except ye repent, ye shall all likewise perish.

Or those eighteen, upon whom the tower in Siloam fell, and slew them, think ye that they were sinners above all men that dwelt in Jerusalem?

I tell you, Nay : but, except ye repent, ye shall all likewise perish.

He spake also this parable : A certain *man* had a fig tree planted in his vineyard ; and he came and sought fruit thereon, and found none.

Then said he unto the dresser of his vineyard, Behold, these three years I come seeking fruit on this fig tree, and find none : cut it down ; why cumbereth it the ground?

And he answering said unto him, Lord, let it alone this year also, till I shall dig about it, and dung *it:* and if it bear fruit, *well*: and if not, *then* after that thou shalt cut it down.

CHAPTER XVI.

THE PARABLES

THE same day went Jesus out of the house, and sat by the sea side.

And great multitudes were gathered together unto Him, so that He went into a ship, and sat ; and the whole multitude stood on the shore.

And He spake many things unto them in parables, saying, Behold, a sower went forth to sow ;

And when he sowed, some *seeds* fell by the way side, and the fowls came and devoured them up :

Some fell upon stony places, where they had not much earth : and forthwith

"Behold a sower went forth to sow."

they sprung up, because they had no deepness of earth:

And when the sun was up, they were scorched: and because they had no root, they withered away.

And some fell among thorns; and the thorns sprung up, and choked them:

But other fell into good ground, and brought forth fruit, some a hundredfold, some sixtyfold, some thirtyfold.

Who hath ears to hear, let him hear.

Another parable put He forth unto them, saying, The kingdom of heaven is likened unto a man which sowed good seed in his field: but while men slept, his enemy came and sowed tares among the wheat, and went his way.

But when the blade was sprung up, and brought forth fruit, then appeared the tares also.

So the servants of the householder came and said unto him, Sir, didst not thou sow good seed in thy field? from whence then hath it tares?

He said unto them, An enemy has done this. The servants said unto him, Wilt thou then that we go and gather them up?

But he said, Nay; lest while ye gather up the tares ye root up also the wheat with them.

Let both grow together until the harvest: and in the time of harvest I will say to the reapers, Gather ye together first the tares, and bind them in bundles to burn them: but gather the wheat into my barn.

And He said, So is the kingdom of God, as if a man should cast seed into the ground; and should sleep, and rise night and day and the seed should spring and grow up, he knoweth not how.

For the earth bringeth forth fruit of herself; first the blade, then the ear, after that the full corn in the ear.

But when the fruit is brought forth, immediately he putteth in the sickle, because the harvest is come.

¶ Another parable put He forth unto them, saying, the kingdom of heaven is like to a grain of mustard seed, which a man took and sowed in his field:

Which indeed is the least of all seeds; but when it is grown, it is the greatest among herbs, and becometh a tree, so that the birds of the air come and lodge in the branches thereof.

¶ Another parable spake He unto them: The kingdom of heaven is like unto leaven, which a woman took, and hid in three measures of meal, till the whole was leavened.

All these things spake Jesus unto the multitude in parables; and without a parable spake He not unto them·

That it might be fulfilled which was spoken by the prophet, saying, I will open my mouth in parables; I will utter things which have been kept secret from the foundation of the world.

Who hath ears to hear, let him hear.

And the disciples came, and said unto Him, Why speakest thou unto them in parables?

He answered and said unto them, Because it is given unto you to know the mysteries of the kingdom of heaven, but to them it is not given.

For whosoever hath, to him shall be given, and he shall have more abundance : but whosoever hath not, from him shall be taken away even that he hath.

Therefore speak I to them in parables : because they seeing see not ; and hearing they hear not, neither do they understand.

And in them is fulfilled the prophecy of Esaias, which saith, By hearing ye shall hear, and shall not understand ; and seeing ye shall see, and shall not perceive :

For this people's heart is waxed gross, and *their* ears are dull of hearing, and their eyes they have closed ; lest at any time they should see with *their* eyes, and hear with *their* ears, and should understand with *their* heart, and should be converted, and I should heal them.

But blessed *are* your eyes, for they see : and your ears for they hear.

For verily I say unto you, That many prophets and righteous *men* have desired to see *those things* which ye see, and have not seen *them ;* and to hear *those things* which ye hear, and have not heard *them.*

Hear ye therefore the parable of the sower.

When any one heareth the word of the kingdom, and understandeth *it* not, then cometh the wicked one, and catcheth away that which was sown in his heart. This is he which received seed by the way side.

But he that received the seed into stony places, the same is he that heareth the word, and anon with joy receiveth it ;

Yet hath he not root in himself, but dureth for a while: for when tribulation or persecution ariseth because of the word, by and by he is offended.

He also that received seed among the thorns is he that heareth the word; and the care of this world, and the deceitfulness of riches, choke the word, and he becometh unfruitful.

But he that received seed into the good ground is he that heareth the word, and understandeth *it;* which also beareth fruit, and bringeth forth some a hundredfold some sixty, some thirty.

And He said unto them, No man, when he hath lighted a candle, covereth it with a vessel, or putteth *it* under a bushel, or under a bed; but setteth *it* on a candlestick, that they which enter in may see the light.

For nothing is secret, that shall not be made manifest; neither *any thing* hid that shall not be known and come abroad.

Take heed therefere how ye hear, and what ye hear.

With what measure ye mete, it shall be measured to you; and unto you that hear, shall more be given.

For whosoever hath, to him shall be given; and whosoever hath not, from him shall be taken even that which he seemeth to have.

And the disciples said Declare unto us the parable of the tares of the field.

He answered and said unto them, He that soweth the good seed is the Son of Man;

The field is the world; the good seed are the children of the kingdom; but the tares are the children of the wicked one;

The enemy that sowed them is the devil; the harvest is the end of the world; and the reapers are the angels.

As therefore the tares are gathered and burned in the fire; so shall it be in the end of this world.

The Son of Man shall send forth His angels, and they shall gather out of His kingdom all things that offend, and them which do iniquity; and shall cast them into a furnace of fire: there shall be wailing and gnashing of teeth.

Then shall the righteous shine forth as the sun in the kingdom of their Father. Who hath ears to hear, let him hear.

Again, the kingdom of heaven is like unto treasure hid in a field; the which when a man hath found, he hideth, and for joy thereof goeth, and selleth all that he hath, and buyeth that field.

Again, the kingdom of heaven is like unto a merchantman, seeking goodly pearls:

Who, when he had found one pearl of great price, went and sold all that he had, and bought it.

Again, the kingdom of heaven is like unto a net, that was cast into the sea, and gathered of every kind:

Which, when it was full, they drew to shore, and sat down, and gathered the good into vessels, but cast the bad away.

So shall it be at the end of the world: the angels shall come forth, and sever the wicked from among the just.

And shall cast them into the furnace of fire: there shall be wailing and gnashing of teeth.

Jesus saith unto them, Have ye understood all

these things? They say unto Him, Yea, Lord.

Then said He unto them, Therefore every scribe *which is* instructed unto the kingdom of heaven, is like unto a man *that is* a householder, which bringeth forth out of his treasure *things* new and old.

And it came to pass, *that* when Jesus had finished these parables, He departed thence.

And the same day when the even was come, when Jesus saw great multitudes about Him, He entered into a ship with His disciples, and gave commandment to depart unto the other side.

And a certain scribe came and said unto Him, Master, I will follow thee whithersoever thou goest.

And Jesus saith unto him, Foxes have holes, and birds of the air *have* nests; but the Son of Man hath not where to lay *His* head.

And He said unto another, Follow me. But he said, Lord, suffer me first to go and bury my father.

Jesus said unto him, Let the dead bury their dead: but go thou and preach the kingdom of God.

And another also said, Lord, I will follow thee; but let me first go bid them farewell, which are at home at my house.

And Jesus said unto him, No man, having put his hand to the plough, and looking back, is fit for the kingdom of God.

CHAPTER XVII.

HE STILLEST THE TEMPEST.

AND the same day, when the even was come, He saith unto them, Let us pass over unto the other side.

"Peace, Be Still."

And when they had sent away the multitude, they took Him even as He was in the ship. And there were also with Him other little ships.

And there arose a great storm of wind, and the waves beat into the ship, so that it was now full.

And He was in the hinder part of the ship asleep on a pillow: and they awake Him, and say unto Him, Master, carest thou not that we perish?

And He arose, and rebuked the wind, and said unto the sea, Peace, be still. And the wind ceased, and there was a great calm.

And He said unto them, Why are ye so fearful? how is it that ye have no faith?

And they feared exceedingly, and said one to another, What manner of man is this, that even the wind and the sea obey Him.

HE CASTETH OUT DEVILS.

AND they came over unto the other side of the sea, into the country of the Gadarenes, which is over against Galilee.

And when He was come out of the ship, immediately there met Him coming out of the tombs, a certain man with an unclean spirit, exceeding fierce, so that no man might pass by that way; which had devils long time, and ware no clothes, neither abode in *any* house, but had *his* dwelling among the tombs.

And no man could bind him, no, not with chains: because that he had been often bound with fetters and chains, and the chains had been plucked asunder by him, and the fetters broken in pieces: neither could any *man* tame him.

And always, night and day, he was in the mountains, and in the tombs, crying, and cutting himself with stones.

But when he saw Jesus afar off, he ran and fell down before Him, and worshipped Him;

And cried with a loud voice, and said, What have I to do with thee, Jesus, *thou* Son of the most high God? Art thou come hither to torment us before the time? I beseech thee, I adjure thee by God, that thou torment me not.

(For He said unto Him, Come out of the man, *thou* unclean spirit. For oftentimes it had caught him: and he was kept bound with chains and fetters; and he brake the bands, and was driven of the devil into the wilderness.)

And Jesus asked him, What is thy name? And he answered, saying, My name *is* Legion: for we are many. (Because many devils were entered into him.)

And they besought Him much that He would not send them away out of the country, and that He would not command them to go out into the deep.

Now there was a good way off from them, nigh unto the mountains, a great herd of swine feeding.

And all the devils besought Him, saying, If thou cast us out, suffer us to go away into the herd of swine, that we may enter into them.

HE PERMITTETH THE DEVILS TO ENTER INTO SWINE.

AND forthwith Jesus gave them leave, and said unto them, Go.

Then went the devils out of the man, and entered into the swine: and, behold, the whole herd of swine ran violently down a steep place into the sea, (they were about two thousand,) and were choked in the sea, and perished.

When they that fed the swine saw what was done, they fled, and went their ways into the city and country, and told every thing, and what was befallen to the possessed of the devils.

And, behold, the whole city went out to meet Jesus, and to see what it was that was done.

And they come to Jesus, and see him that was possessed with the devils, and had the legion, sitting at the feet of Jesus, clothed, and in his right mind : and they were afraid.

They also which saw *it*, told them by what means he that was possessed of the devils was healed, and *also* concerning the swine.

Then the whole multitude of the country of the Gadarenes round about, besought Jesus that He would depart out of their coasts; (for t h e y were taken with great fear :) and He went up into the ship and returned back again.

And when **He** was come into the ship, the man out of whom the devils were departed, besought Him that he might be with Him:

Howbeit Jesus suffered him not, but saith unto him, Go h o m e to thy friends, and tell them how great things the Lord hath done for thee, and hath had compassion on thee.

And he departed, and began to publish in Decapolis and throughout the whole city how great things

Jesus had done for him: and all *men* did marvel.

And when Jesus was passed over again by ship unto the other side. into His own city, the people *gladly* received Him: for they were all waiting for Him.

HE HEALETH THE WOMAN, AND RAISETH FROM DEATH JAIRUS' DAUGHTER,

AND, behold, there came a man named Jairus, and he was a ruler of the synagogue; and he fell down at Jesus' feet, and besought Him that He would come into his house:

For he had one only daughter, about twelve years of age, and she lay a dying. But as He went the people thronged Him.

¶ And a woman having an issue of blood twelve years, which had spent all her living upon physicians, neither could be healed of any.

Came behind *Him*, and touched the border of His garment: and immediately her issue of blood stanched.

And Jesus said, Who touched me? When all denied, Peter and they that were with Him said, Master the multitude throng thee and press *thee*, and sayest thou, Who touched me?

And Jesus said, Somebody hath touched me: for I perceive that virtue is gone out of me.

And when the woman saw that she was not hid, she came trembling, and falling down before Him, she declared unto Him before all the people for what cause she had touched Him, and how she was healed immediately.

And He said unto her,

"Daughter, be of good comfort: thy faith hath made thee whole; go in peace."

And her spirit came again.

Daughter, be of good comfort: thy faith hath made thee whole; go in peace.

While He yet spake, there cometh one from the ruler of the synagogue's *house*, saying to him, Thy daughter is dead; trouble not the master.

But when Jesus heard *it*, He answered him, saying, Fear not: believe only, and she shall be made whole.

And when He came into the house, He suffered no man to go in save Peter, and James, and John, and the father and the mother of the maiden.

And all wept, and bewailed her: but He said, Weep not; she is not dead, but sleepeth.

And they laughed Him to scorn, knowing that she was dead.

But when He had put them all out, He taketh the father and the mother of the damsel, and them that were with Him, and entereth in where the damsel was lying.

And He took her by the hand, and called, saying, Talitha cumi! (which is, being interpreted,) Damsel, I say unto thee, arise!

And her spirit came again, and straightway she arose and walked: for she was *of the age* of twelve years. And He commanded that something should be given her to eat.

And her parents were astonished with a great astonishment; but He charged them that they should tell no man what was done.

GIVETH SIGHT TO TWO BLIND MEN.

And when Jesus departed thence, two blind men followed Him, crying and saying, *Thou* Son of David have mercy on us!

And when He was come into the house, the blind men came to Him: and Jesus saith unto them, Believe ye that I am able to do this: They said unto Him, Yea, Lord.

Then touched He their eyes, saying, According to your faith be it unto you.

And their eyes were opened; and Jesus straitly charged them, saying, See *that* no man know *it*.

But they, when they had departed, spread abroad His fame in all that country.

HEALETH A DUMB MAN POSSESSED OF A DEVIL.

As they went out, behold, they brought to Him a dumb man possessed of a devil.

And when the devil was cast out the dumb spake: and the multitudes marvelled, saying, It was never so seen in Israel.

But the Pharisees said, He casteth out devils through the prince of the devils.

And Jesus went about all the cities and villages, teaching in their synagogues, and preaching the gospel of the kingdom, and healing every sickness and every disease among the people.

But when He saw the multitudes, He was moved with compassion on them. because they fainted, and were scattered abroad, as sheep having no shepherd.

Then saith He unto His disciples, The harvest truly *is* plenteous, but the labourers *are* few.

Pray ye therefore the Lord of the harvest, that He will send forth labourers into His harvest.

And Jesus went about all the cities and villages, teaching in their synagogues, and preaching the gospel of the kingdom, and healing every sickness and every disease among the people.

CHAPTER XVIII.

CHRIST SENDETH OUT HIS TWELVE APOSTLES.

AND when He had called unto *Him* His twelve disciples, He gave them power *against* unclean spirits, to cast them out, and to heal all manner of sickness and all manner of disease.

These twelve Jesus sent forth, and commanded them, saying, Go not into the way of the Gentiles, and into *any* city of the Samaritans enter ye not :

But go rather to the lost sheep of the house of Israel.

And as ye go, preach, saying, the kingdom of heaven is at hand.

Heal the sick, cleanse the lepers, raise the dead, cast out devils : freely ye have received, freely give.

Provide neither gold, nor silver, nor brass in your purses ;

Nor scrip for *your* journey, neither two coats, neither shoes, nor yet staves : for the workman is worthy of his meat.

And into whatsoever city or town ye shall enter, inquire who in it is worthy ; and there abide till ye go thence.

And when ye come into a house, salute it.

And if the house be worthy, let your peace come upon it ; but if it be not worthy, let your peace return to you.

And whosoever shall not receive you, nor hear your words, when ye depart out of that house or city, shake off the dust of your feet.

Verily I say unto you, It shall be more tolerable for the land of Sodom and Gomorrah in the day of judgment, than for that city.

Behold, I send you forth as sheep in the midst of wolves: be ye therefore wise as serpents, and harmless as doves.

But beware of men: for they will deliver you up to the councils, and they will scourge you in their synagogues;

And ye shall be brought before governors and kings for my sake, for a testimony against them and the Gentiles.

But when they deliver you up, take no thought how or what ye shall speak: for it shall be given you in that same hour what ye shall speak.

For it is not ye that speak but the spirit of your Father which speaketh in you.

And the brother shall deliver up the brother to death, and the father the child: and the children shall rise up against *their* parents, and cause them to be put to death.

And ye shall be hated of all *men* for my name's sake: but he that endureth to the end shall be saved.

But when they persecute you in this city, flee ye into another: for verily I say unto you, Ye shall not have gone over the cities of Israel, till the Son of Man be come.

The disciple is not above *his* master, nor the servant above his lord.

It is enough for the disciple that he be as his master, and the servant as his lord. If they have called the master of the house Beelzebub, how much more *shall they call* them of his household?

Fear them not therefore: for there is nothing covered that shall not be revealed; and hid, that shall not be known.

What I tell you in darkness, *that* speak ye in light: and what ye hear in the ear, *that* preach ye upon the housetops.

And fear not them which kill the body, but are not able to kill the soul: but rather fear Him which is able to destroy both soul and body in hell.

Are not two sparrows sold for a farthing? and one of them shall not fall on the ground without your Father.

But the very hairs of your head are all numbered.

Fear ye not therefore, ye are of more value than many sparrows.

Whosoever therefore shall confess me before men, him will I confess also before my Father which is in heaven.

But whosoever shall deny me before men, him will I also deny before my Father which is in heaven.

Think not that I am come to send peace on earth: I came not to send peace, but a sword.

For I am come to set a man at variance against his father, and the daughter against her mother, and the daughter-in-law against her mother-in-law.

And a man's foes *shall be* they of his own household.

He that loveth father or mother more than me is not worthy of me: and he that loveth son or daughter more than me is not worthy of me.

And he that taketh not his cross and followeth after me, is not worthy of me.

He that findeth his life shall lose it: and he that loseth his life for my sake shall find it.

He that receiveth you receiveth me; and he that receiveth me receiveth Him that sent me.

He that receiveth a

prophet in the name of a prophet shall receive a prophet's reward; and he that receiveth a righteous man in the name of a righteous man shall receive a righteous man's reward.

And whosoever shall give to drink unto one of these little ones a cup of cold *water* only in the name of a disciple, verily I say unto you, he shall in no wise lose his reward.

¶ And it came to pass when Jesus had made an end of commanding His twelve disciples, He departed thence to teach and to preach in their cities.

And they went out and preached that men should repent.

And they cast out many devils, and anointed with oil many that were sick, and healed *them*.

CHAPTER XIX.

WHEREFORE JOHN BAPTIST WAS BEHEADED.

AT that time Herod the tetrarch heard of the fame of Jesus; (for His name was spread abroad;) and he said, That John the Baptist was risen from the dead, and therefore mighty works do shew forth themselves in him.

Others said, This is Elias. And others said, That it is a prophet, or as one of the prophets.

But when Herod heard *thereof*, he said, It is John, whom I beheaded: he is risen from the dead.

For Herod himself had sent forth and laid hold upon John, and bound him in prison for Herodias' sake, his brother Philip's wife; for he had married her.

For John had said unto

And the damsel gave it to her mother.

Herod, It is not lawful for thee to have thy brother's wife.

Therefore Herodias had a quarrel against him, and would have killed him; but she could not:

For Herod feared John, knowing that he was a just man and a holy, and observed him: and when he heard him, he did many things, and heard him gladly.

And when a convenient day was come, that Herod on his birthday made a supper to his lords, high captains, and chief *estates* of Galilee;

And when the daughter of the said Herodias came in and danced, and pleased Herod and them that sat with him, the king said unto the damsel, Ask of me whatsoever thou wilt, and I will give *it* thee.

And he sware unto her, Whatsoever thou shalt ask of me, I will give *it* thee, unto the half of my kingdom.

And she went forth, and said unto her mother, What shall I ask? And she said, The head of John the Baptist.

And she came in straightway with haste unto the king, and asked, saying, I will that thou give me by and by in a charger the head of John the Baptist.

And the king was exceeding sorry; *yet* for his oath's sake, and for their sakes which sat with him, he would not reject her.

And immediately the king sent an executioner, and commanded his head to be brought: and he went and beheaded him in the prison.

And brought his head in a charger, and gave it to the damsel; and the damsel gave it to her mother.

And when his disciples heard *of it*, they came and took up his corpse, and laid it in a tomb.

And the apostles gathered themselves together unto Jesus, and told Him all things, both what they had done, and what they had taught.

And He said unto them, Come ye yourselves apart into a desert place, and rest a while: for there were many coming and going, and they had no leisure so much as to eat.

And He took them, by ship privately into a desert place belonging to the city called Bethsaida.

And the people saw them departing, and many knew Him, and ran afoot thither out of all cities, and outwent them, and came together unto Him.

And Jesus, when He came out, saw much people, and was moved with compassion toward them, because they were as sheep not having a shepherd: and He began to teach them many things and healed them that had need of healing.

And when the day began to wear away, and was now far spent, His disciples came unto Him, saying, This is a desert place, and now the time *is* far passed:

Send the multitude away, that they may go into the towns and country round about, and lodge and buy themselves bread: for they have nothing to eat; for we are here in a desert place.

But Jesus said unto them, They need not depart; give ye them to eat. And they say unto Him, Shall we go and buy fwo hundred pennyworth of bread, and give them to eat.

And they did all eat, and were filled.

And He saith unto Philip, Whence shall we buy bread that these may eat? (And this He said to prove him: for He Himself knew what He would do.)

Philip answered Him, Two hundred pennyworth of bread is not sufficient for them, that every one of them may take a little.

He saith unto them, How many loaves have ye? go and see. And when they knew, one of His disciples, Andrew, Simon Peter's brother, saith unto Him.

There is a lad here, which hath five barley loaves and two small fishes: but what are they among so many? And they said, We have no more but five loaves and two fishes: except we should go and buy meat for all this people.

(For they were about five thouand men.)

He said, Bring them hither to me.

And He commanded them to make the multitude sit down by fifties in a company, upon the green grass. Now there was much grass in the place. So the men sat down, in ranks, by hundreds, and by fifties, in number about five thousand.

And Jesus took the five loaves, and the two fishes, and looking up to heaven, He blessed them, and brake; and when He had given thanks, He distributed to His disciples to set before the multitude; and the two fishes, likewise divided He among them all, as much as they would.

And they did all eat, and were filled.

When they were filled, He said unto His disciples, Gather the fragments that remain, that nothing be lost.

Therefore they gathered *them* together, and filled twelve baskets full with the fragments of the five barley loaves, and of the fishes, which remained over and above unto them that had eaten.

And they that had eaten were about five thousand men, beside women and children.

Then those men, when they had seen the miracle that Jesus did, said, This is of a truth that prophet that should come into the world.

When Jesus therefore perceived that they would come and take Him by force, to make Him a king, straightway He constrained His disciples to get into a ship, and to go before Him unto the other side, unto Bethsaida, while He sent away the people.

And His disciples went down unto the sea, and entered into a ship, and went over the sea toward Capernaum.

And when He had sent the multitudes away, He went up into a mountain apart to pray, Himself alone.

And when the evening was come, the ship was in the midst of the sea, and He alone on the land.

And the sea arose by reason of a great wind that blew. And it was now dark, and Jesus was not come to them,

But the ship was in the midst of the sea, tossed with waves.

CHRIST WALKETH ON THE SEA.

AND He saw them toiling in rowing; for the wind was contrary unto them.

So when they had rowed about five-and-twenty or thirty furlongs, and about

the fourth watch of the night, He cometh unto them, walking upon the sea, and would have passed by them.

But when they saw Him walking upon the sea, and drawing nigh unto the ship, they were troubled, saying, It is a spirit! and they cried out for fear: for they all saw Him, and were troubled.

And immediately He talked with them, and saith unto them, Be of good cheer: it is I; be not afraid.

And Peter answered Him and said, Lord, if it be thou, bid me come unto thee on the water.

And He said, Come. And when Peter was come down out of the ship, he walked on the water to go to Jesus.

And when he saw the wind boisterous, he was afraid; and beginning to sink, he cried, saying, Lord, save me!

And immediately Jesus stretched forth *His* hand, and caught him, and said unto him, O thou of little faith, wherefore didst thou doubt?

Then they willingly received Him into the ship, and the wind ceased; and immediately the ship was at the land whither they went.

Then they that were in the ship came and worshipped Him, saying, Of a truth thou art the Son of God!

And they were sore amazed in themselves beyond measure, and wondered. For they considered not *the miracle* of the loaves; for their heart was hardened.

And they came into the land of Gennesaret. And when they were come out of the ship, straightway the men of that place knew Him.

And ran through that whole region round about, and began to carry about in beds those that were sick, where they heard He was.

And whithersoever He entered, into villages, or cities, or country, they laid the sick in the streets, and besought Him that they might touch if it were but the border of His garment: and as many as touched Him were made perfectly whole.

CHAPTER XX.

CHRIST HIMSELF THE BREAD OF LIFE TO BELIEVERS.

THE day following, when the people, which stood on the other side of the sea, saw that there was none other boat there, save that one wherein His disciples were entered, and that Jesus went not with His disciples into the boat, but *that* His disciples were gone away alone;

Howbeit there came other boats from Tiberias nigh unto the place where they did eat bread, after that the Lord had given thanks;

When the people therefore saw that Jesus was not there, neither His disciples, they also took shipping, and came to Capernaum, seeking for Jesus.

And when they had found Him on the other side of the sea, they said unto Him, Rabbi, when camest thou hither?

Jesus answered them and said, Verily, verily, I say unto you, Ye seek me, not because ye saw the miracles, but because ye did eat of the loaves, and were filled.

Labour not for the meat

which perisheth, but for that meat which endureth unto everlasting life, which the Son of Man shall give unto you: for Him hath God the Father sealed,

Then said they unto Him, What shall we do, that we might work the works of God?

Jesus answered and said unto them, This is the work of God, that ye believe on Him whom He hath sent.

They said therefore unto Him, What sign shewest thou then, that we may see, and believe thee? what dost thou work?

Our fathers did eat manna in the desert; as it is written, He gave them bread from heaven to eat.

Then Jesus said nnto them, Verily, verily, I say unto you, Moses gave not that bread from heaven; but my Father giveth you the true bread from heaven.

For the bread of God is He which cometh dowu from heaven, and giveth life unto the world.

Then said they unto Him, Lord, evermore give us this bread.

And Jesus said unto them, I am the bread of life: he that cometh to me shall never hunger; and he that believeth on me shall never thirst.

But I said unto you, That ye also have seen me and believe not.

All that the Father giveth me shall come to me: and him that cometh to me I will in no wise cast out.

For I came down from heaven, not to do mine own will, but the will of Him that sent me.

And this is the Father's will which hath sent me, that of all which He hath given me I should lose nothing, but should raise it up again at the last day.

And this is the will of Him that sent me, that every one which seeth the Son, and believeth on Him, may have everlasting life: and I will raise him up at the last day.

The Jews then murmured at Him because He said, I am the bread which came down from heaven,

And they said is not this Jesus, the son of Joseph, whose father and mother we know? how is it then that He saith, I came down from heaven?

Jesus therefore answered and said unto them, Murmur not among yourselves.

No man can come to me, except the Father which hath sent me draw him: and I will raise him up at the last day.

It is written in the prophets, And they shall be all taught of God. Every man therefore that hath heard, and learned of the Father, cometh unto me.

Not that any man hath seen the Father, save He which is of God, He hath seen the Father.

Verily, verily, I say unto you, He that believeth on me hath everlasting life.

I am the bread of life,

Your fathers did eat manna in the wilderness, and are dead.

This is the bread which cometh down from heaven, that a man may eat thereof, and not die.

I am the living bread which came down from heaven: if any man eat of this bread, he shall live for ever: and the bread that I will give is my flesh, which I will give for the life of the world,

The Jews therefore strove

among themselves, saying, How can this man give us *His* flesh to eat?

Then Jesus said unto them, Verily, verily, I say unto you, Except ye eat the flesh of the Son of man, and drink His blood, ye have no life in you.

Whoso eateth my flesh, and drinketh my blood, hath eternal life ; and I will raise him up at the last day.

For my flesh is meat indeed, and my blood is drink indeed.

He that eateth my flesh, and drinketh my blood, dwelleth in me, and I in him.

As the living Father hath sent me, and I live by the Father: so he that eateth me, even he shall live by me:

This is that bread which came down from heaven : not as your fathers did eat manna and are dead : he that eateth of this bread shall live for ever.

These things said He in the synagogue, as He taught in Capernaum.

Many of His disciples, when they heard *this*, said, This is a hard saying ; who can hear it?

When Jesus knew in Himself that His disciples murmured at it, He said unto them, Doth this offend you?

What and if ye shall see the Son of Man ascend up where He was before?

It is the Spirit that quickeneth ; the flesh profiteth nothing : the words that I speak unto you, *they* are spirit, and *they* are life.

But there are some of you who believe not. For Jesus knew from the beginning who they were that believed not, and who should betray Him.

And He said, Therefore

said I unto you, that no man can come unto me, except it were given unto him by my Father.

¶ From that *time* many of His disciples went back, and walked no more with Him.

Then said Jesus unto the twelve, Will ye also go away?

Then Simon Peter answered Him, Lord, to whom shall we go? thou hast the words of eternal life.

And we believe and are sure that thou art that Christ, the Son of the living God,

Jesus answered them, Have not I chosen you twelve, and one of you is a devil:

He spake of Judas Iscariot, *the son* of Simon: for he it was that should betray Him, being one of the twelve.

CHAPTER XXI.

WHAT DEFILETH THE MAN.

THEN came together unto Him the Pharisees, and certain of the scribes, which came from Jerusalem.

And when they saw some of His disciples eat bread with defiled, that is to say with unwashen hands, they found fault.

For the Pharisees, and all the Jews, except they wash *their* hands oft, eat not, holding the tradition of the elders.

And *when they come* from the market, except they wash, they eat not. And many other things there be, which they have received to hold, *as* the washing of cups, and pots, brazen vessels, and of tables.

Then the Pharisees and scribes asked Him, Why walk not thy disciples according to the tradition of the elders, but eat bread with unwashen hands?

He answered and said unto them, Well hath Esaias prophesied of you hypocrites, as it is written, This people honoureth me with *their* lips, but their heart is far from me.

Howbeit in vain do they worship me, teaching *for* doctrines the commandments of men.

For laying aside the commandment of God, ye hold the tradition of men, *as* the washing of pots and cups: and many other such like things ye do.

And He said unto them, Full well ye reject the commandment of God, that ye may keep your own tradition.

For Moses said, Honour thy father and thy mother; and, Whoso curseth father or mother, let him die the death:

But ye say, If a man shall say to his father or mother, *It is* Corban, that is to say, a gift, by whatsoever thou mightest be profited by me; *he shall be free.*

And ye suffer him no more to do aught for his father or mother;

Making the word of God of none effect through your tradition, which ye have delivered: and many such like things do ye.

¶ And when He had called all the people *unto Him*, He said unto them, Hearken unto me every one *of you*, and understand:

There is nothing from without a man, that entering into him can defile him: but the things which come out of him, those are **they** that defile the man.

If any man have ears to hear, let him hear.

Then came His disciples, and said unto Him, Knowest thou that the Pharisees were offended, after they heard this saying?

But He answered and said, Every plant which my heavenly Father hath not planted shall be rooted up.

Let them alone: they be blind leaders of the blind. And if the blind lead the blind, both shall fall into the ditch.

Then answered Peter and said unto Him, Declare unto us this parable.

And Jesus said, Are ye also yet without understanding?

Do ye not yet understand, that whatsoever entereth in at the mouth goeth into the belly, and is cast out into the draught?

But those things which proceed out of the mouth come forth from the heart; and they defile the man.

For out of the heart proceed evil thoughts, murders, adulteries, fornications, thefts, false witness, blasphemies:

These are *the things* which defile a man: but to eat with unwashen hands defileth not a man.

HE HEALETH THE SYROPHŒNICIAN WOMAN'S DAUGHTER

AND from thence He arose, and went into the borders of Tyre and Sidon, and entered into a house, and would have no man know *it*: but He could not be hid.

And, behold, a woman of Canaan came out of the same coasts, and cried unto Him, saying, Have mercy on me, O Lord. *thou* Son of David; my daughter is

"Great is thy faith: be it unto thee even as thou wilt."

grievously vexed with a devil.

The woman was a Greek, a Syrophœnician by nation; and she besought Him that He would cast forth the devil out of her daughter.

But He answered her not a word. And His disciples came and besought him, saying, Send her away; for she crieth after us.

But He answered and said, I am not sent but unto the lost sheep of the house of Israel.

Then came she and worshipped Him, saying, Lord, help me.

But He answered and said, It is not meet to take the children's bread, and to cast *it* to dogs.

And she said, Truth, Lord: yet the dogs eat of the crumbs which fall from their master's table.

Then Jesus answered and said unto her, O woman, great *is* thy faith: be it unto thee even as thou wilt. And her daughter was made whole from that very hour.

And when she was come to her house, she found the devil gone out, and her daughter laid upon tne bed.

HE CURETH A DEAF AND STAMMERING ONE.

AND again, departing from the coasts of Tyre and Sidon, He came unto the sea of Galilee, through the midst of the coasts of Decapolis.

And they bring unto Him one that was deaf, and had an impediment in his speech; and they beseech Him to put His hand upon him.

And He took him aside from the multitude, and put His fingers into his ears, and He spit, and touched his tongue;

And looking up to heaven,

He sighed, and saith unto him, Ephphatha, that is, Be opened.

And straightway his eyes were opened, and the string of his tongue was loosed, and he spake plain,

And He charged them that they should tell no man: but the more He charged them, so much the more a great deal they published *it:*

And were beyond measure astonished, saying, He hath done all things well: He maketh both the deaf to hear and the dumb to speak.

And Jesus departed from thence, and came nigh unto the sea of Galilee; and went up into a mountain, and sat down there.

And great multitudes came unto Him, having with them *those that were* lame, blind, dumb, maimed, and many others, and cast them down at Jesus' feet; and He healed them:

Insomuch that the multitude wondered, when they saw the dumb to speak, the maimed to be whole, the lame to walk, and the blind to see: and they glorified the God of Israel.

¶ Then Jesus called His disciples *unto Him*, and said, I have compassion on the multitude, because they continue with me now three days, and have nothing to eat: and I will not send them away fasting, lest they faint in the way.

And His disciples said unto Him, Whence should we have so much bread in the wilderness, as to fill so great a multitude?

And Jesus saith unto them, How many loves have ye? And they said, Seven, and a few little fishes.

And He commanded the

"I am the living bread which came down from heaven."

multitude to sit down on the ground.

And **He** took the seven loaves and the fishes, and gave thanks, and b r a k e *them*, and gave to His disciples. and the disciples to the multitude.

And they did all eat, and were filled : and they took up of the broken *meat* that was left seven baskets full.

And they that did eat were four thousand men, beside women and children.

CHAPTER XXII.

THE PHARISEES REQUIRE A SIGN.

AND He sent away the multitude, and took ship, and came into the coasts of Magdala.

And the Pharisees came forth, and began to question with Him, seeking of Him a sign from heaven, tempting Him.

He answered and said unto them, When it is evening ye say, *It will be* fair weather : for the sky is red.

And in t h e morning, *It will be* foul weather to-day ; for the sky is red and lowering. O *ye* hypocrites, ye can discern the face of the sky ; but can ye not *discern* the s i g n s of the times ?

A wicked and adulterous generation seeketh after a sign : and there shall no sign be given unto it, but the sign of the prophet Jonas.

And He sighed deeply in his spirit, and saith, Why doth this generation seek after a sign ? verily, I say unto you, There shall no sign be given unto this generation.

And He left them, and entering into the ship again d e p a r t e d to the o t h e r side.

¶ Now *the disciples* had forgotten to take bread, neither had they in the ship with them more than one loaf.

And He charged them, saying, Take heed, beware of the leaven of the Pharisees and of the leaven of Herod.

And they reasoned among themselves, saying, *It is* because we have no bread.

And when Jesus knew *it*, He saith unto them, Why reason ye, because ye have no bread? perceive ye not yet, neither understand? have ye your heart yet hardened?

Having eyes, see ye not? and having ears, hear ye not? and do ye not remember?

When I brake the five loaves among the five thousand, how many baskets full of fragments took ye up? They say unto Him, Twelve.

And when the seven among four thousand, how many baskets full of fragments took ye up? And they said, Seven.

And He said unto them, How is it that ye do not understand?

How is it that ye do not understand that I spake *it* not to you concerning bread, that ye should beware of the leaven of the Pharisees and of the Sadducees?

Then understood they how that He bade *them* not beware of the leaven of bread, but of the doctrine of the Pharisees and of the Sadducees.

HE GIVETH A BLIND MAN SIGHT.

AND He cometh to Bethsaida; and they bring a blind man unto Him, and besought Him to touch him.

And He took the blind

And He took the blind man by the hand, and led him out of the town.

man by the hand, and led him out of the town; and when He had spit on his eyes, and put His hands upon him, He asked him if he saw aught.

And he looked up, and said, I see men as trees, walking.

After that He put *His* hands again upon his eyes, and made him look up; and he was restored, and saw every man clearly.

And He sent him away to his house, saying, Neither go into the town, nor tell *it* to any in the town.

PETER'S CONFESSION OF CHRIST.

AND Jesus went out, and His disciples, into the towns of Cesarea Philippi: and by the way He asked His disciples, saying unto them, Whom do men say that I am?

And they said, Some *say that thou art* John the Baptist; some, Elias; and others, Jeremias, or one of the prophets.

He saith unto them, But whom say ye that I am?

And Simon Peter answered and said, Thou art the Christ, the Son of the living God.

And Jesus answered and said unto him, Blessed art thou, Simon Bar-jona: for flesh and blood hath not revealed *it* unto thee, but my Father which is in heaven.

And I say also unto thee, That thou art Peter, and upon this rock I will build my church; and the gates of hell shall not prevail against it.

And I will give unto

thee the keys of the kingdom of heaven: and whatsoever thou shalt bind on earth shall be bound in heaven: and whatsoever thou shalt loose on earth shall be loosed in heaven.

Then charged He His disciples that they should tell no man that He was Jesus the Christ.

HE FORESHOWETH HIS DEATH.

From that time forth began Jesus to shew unto His disciples, how that He must go unto Jerusalem, and suffer many things of the elders and chief priests and scribes, and be killed, and be raised again the third day.

Then Peter took Him, and began to rebuke Him, saying, Be it far from thee, Lord: this shall not be unto thee.

But when He had turned about and looked on His disciples He rebuked Peter, saying, Get thee behind me, Satan: for thou savourest not the things that be of God, but the things that be of men.

¶ And when He had called the people *unto Him* with His disciples also, He said unto them, Whosoever will come after me, let him deny himself, and take up his cross, and follow me.

For whosoever will save his life shall lose it; but whosoever shall lose his life for my sake and the gospel's the same shall save it.

For what shall it profit a man, if he shall gain the whole world, and lose his own soul?

Or what shall a man give in exchange for his soul?

For the Son of man shall come in the glory of His Father with His angels; and then He shall reward every man according to his works.

Verily, I say unto you, There be some standing here, which shall not taste of death, till they see the Son of man coming in His kingdom.

CHAPTER XXIII.

THE TRANSFIGURATION OF JESUS.

AND after six days Jesus taketh Peter, James, and John his brother, and bringeth them up into a high mountain apart.

And was transfigured before them: and His face did shine as the sun, and His raiment was white as the light.

And, behold, there appeared unto them Moses and Elias talking with Him.

Then answered Peter and said unto Jesus, Lord, it is good for us to be here: if thou wilt, let us make here three tabernacles; one for thee, one for Moses, and one for Elias.

While he yet spake, behold, a bright cloud overshadowed them: and behold a voice out of the cloud, which said, This is my beloved Son, in whom I am well pleased; hear ye Him.

And when the disciples heard *it*, they fell on their face and were sore afraid.

And Jesus came and touched them, and said, Arise, and be not afraid.

And when they had lifted up their eyes, they saw no man, save Jesus only.

And as they came down from the mountain Jesus charged them, saying, Tell the vision to no man until the Son of Man be risen again from the dead.

And they kept that saying with themselves, questioning one with another what the rising from the dead should mean.

And His disciples asked Him, saying, Why then say the scribes that Elias must first come?

And Jesus answered and said unto them, Elias truly shall first come, and restore all things.

But I say unto you, That Elias is come already, and they knew him not, but have done unto him whatsoever they listed. Likewise shall also the Son of Man suffer of them.

Then the disciples understood that He spake unto them of John the Baptist.

¶ And it came to pass, that on the next day, when they were come down from the hill, much people met Him.

And when He came to *His* disciples, He saw a great multitude about them, and the scribes questioning with them.

And straightway all the people, when they beheld Him, were greatly amazed, and running to *Him* saluted Him.

And He asked the scribes, What question ye with them?

And one of the multitude answered and said, Master, I have brought unto thee my son, which hath a dumb spirit;

And wheresoever he taketh him, he teareth him; and he foameth, and gnasheth with his teeth, and pineth away: and I spake to thy disciples that they should cast him out; and they could not.

"This is my beloved Son, in whom I am well pleased; hear ye Him."

He answereth him, and saith, O faithless generation, how long shall I be with you? how long shall I suffer you? bring him unto me.

And they brought him unto Him: and when He saw him, straightway the spirit tare him; and he fell on the ground, and wallowed foaming.

And He asked his father, How long is it ago since this came unto him? And he said, Of a child.

And ofttimes it hath cast him into the fire, and into the waters, to destroy him: but if thou canst do any thing, have compassion on us, and help us.

Jesus said unto him, If thou canst believe, all things *are* possible to him that believeth.

And straightway the father of the child cried out, and said with tears, Lord, I believe; help thou mine unbelief.

When Jesus saw that the people came running together, He rebuked the foul spirit, saying unto him, *Thou* dumb and deaf spirit, I charge thee, come out of him, and enter no more into him.

And *the spirit* cried, and rent him sore and came out of him: and he was as one dead; insomuch that many said, he is dead.

But Jesus took him by the hand and lifted him up; and he arose.

And they were all amazed at the mighty power of God.

And when He was come into the house, His disciples asked Him privately, Why could not we cast him out?

And Jesus said unto them, Because of your unbelief: for verily I say unto you, If ye have faith as a grain of mustard seed, ye shall say unto this mountain, Remove hence to yonder place; and it shall remove: and nothing shall be impossible unto you.

Howbeit this kind goeth not out but by prayer and fasting.

¶ After these things Jesus departed thence and passed through Galilee; for He would not walk in Jewry, because the Jews sought to kill Him.

And while they abode in Galilee, Jesus said unto them, The Son of Man shall be betrayed into the hands of men:

And they shall kill Him, and the third day He shall be raised again. And they were exceeding sorry.

But they understood not that saying, and were afraid to ask Him.

And when they were come to Capernaum, they that received tribute *money* came to Peter, and said, Doth not your master pay tribute?

He saith, Yes. And when he was come into the house, Jesus prevented him, saying. What thinketh thou, Simon? of whom do the kings of the earth take custom or tribute? of their own children or of strangers?

Peter saith unto Him, Of strangers. Jesus saith unto him, Then are the children free.

Notwithstanding, lest we should offend them, go thou to the sea, and cast a hook, and take up the fish that first cometh up; and when thou hast opened his mouth, thou shalt find a piece of money: that take, and

The sea of Galilee, or Tiberias.

give unto them for me and thee.

And being in the house He asked them, What was it that ye disputed among yourselves by the way?

But they held their peace: for by the way they had disputed among themselves who *should be* the greatest.

And He sat down, and called the twelve, and saith unto them, If any man desire to be first, *the same* shall be last of all, and servant of all.

And He took a child, and set him in the midst of them: and when He had taken him in His arms, he said unto them,

Verily I say unto you, E x c e p t ye be converted, and become as little children, ye shall not enter into the kingdom of heaven.

Whosoever t h e r e f o r e shall humble himself as this little child, the s a m e is greatest in the kingdom of heaven.

And whoso shall receive one such little child in my name receiveth me.

But whoso shall offend one of these little ones which believe in me, it were better for him t h a t a millstone were hanged about his neck and *that* he were drowned in the depth of the sea.

And John answered him, saying Master, we saw one casting out devils in thy name, and he followeth not us; and we forbade him, because he followeth not us.

But Jesus said, Forbid him not: for there is no man which shall do a miracle in my name that can lightly speak evil of me.

For he that is not against us is on our part.

For whosoever shall give you a cup of water to drink in my name, because ye belong to Christ, verily I say unto you, he shall not lose his reward.

Woe unto the world because of offences! for it must needs be that offences come; but woe to that man by whom the offence cometh!

Wherefore if thy hand or thy foot offend thee, cut them off, and cast *them* from thee; it is better for thee to enter into life halt or maimed, rather than having two hands or two feet to be cast into everlasting fire.

And if thine eye offend thee, pluck it out, and cast *it* from thee: it is better for thee to enter into life with one eye, rather than having two eyes to be cast into hell fire.

Where their worm dieth not, and the fire is not quenched.

For every one shall be salted with fire, and every sacrifice shall be salted with salt.

Salt *is* good: but if the salt have lost its saltness, wherewith will ye season it? Have salt in yourselves, and have peace one with another.

Take heed that ye despise not one of these little ones; for I say unto you, That in heaven their angels do always behold the face of my Father which is in heaven.

For the Son of Man is come to save that which was lost.

How think ye? if a man have a hundred sheep, and one of them be gone astray, doth he not leave the ninety and nine, and goeth into the mountains, and seeketh that which is gone astray?

And if so be that he find it, verily I say unto you, he rejoiceth more of that *sheep*, than of the ninety

"Verily I say unto you, Except ye be converted, and become as little children, ye shall not enter into the kingdom of heaven."

and nine which went not astray.

Even so it is not the will of your Father which is in heaven, that one of these little ones should perish.

¶ Moreover if thy brother shall trespass against thee, go and tell him his fault between thee and him alone: if he shall hear thee, thou hast gained thy brother.

But if he will not hear *thee, then* take with thee one or two more, that in the mouth of two or three witnesses every word may be established.

And if he shall neglect to hear them, tell *it* unto the church : but if he neglect to hear the church. let him be unto thee as a heathen man and a publican.

Verily I say unto you, Whatsoever ye shall bind on earth shall be bound in heaven ; and whatsoever ye shall loose on earth shall be loosed in heaven.

Again I say unto you, That if two of you shall agree on earth as touching any thing that they shall ask, it shall be done for them of my Father which is in heaven.

For where two or three are gathered together in my name, there am I in the midst of them.

Then came Peter to Him, and said, Lord, how oft shall my brother sin against me, and I forgive him ? till seven times ?

Jesus saith unto him, I say not unto thee, Until seven times : but until seventy times seven.

Therefore is the kingdom of heaven likened unto a certain king, whioh would take account of his servants.

And when he had begun to reckon, one was brought

unto him which owed him ten thousand talents.

But forasmuch as he had not to pay, his lord commanded him to be sold, and his wife and children, and all that he had, and payment to be made.

The servant therefore fell down and worshipped him, saying, Lord, have patience with me, and I will pay thee all,

Then the lord of that servant was moved with compassion, and loosed him and forgave him the debt.

But the same servant went out, and found one of his fellow servants, which owed him a hundred pence: and he laid hands on him, and took *him* by the throat, saying, Pay me that thou owest.

And his fellow servant fell down at his feet, and besought him, saying, Have patience with me and I will pay thee all.

And he would not: but went and cast him into prison, till he should pay the debt.

So when his fellow servants saw what was done, they were very sorry, and came and told unto their lord all that was done.

Then his lord, after that he had called him, said unto him, O thou wicked servant, I forgave thee all that debt, because thou desiredst me:

Shouldest not thou also have had compassion on thy fellow servant, even as I had pity on thee?

And his lord was wroth, and delivered him to the tormentors, till he should pay all that was due unto him.

So likewise shall my heavenly Father do also unto you, if ye from your hearts forgive not every one his brother their trespasses.

CHAPTER XXIV

CHRIST SENDETH OUT SEVENTY OTHER DISCIPLES.

AFTER these things the Lord appointed other seventy also, and sent them two and two before His face into every city and place, whither He Himself would come.

Therefore said He unto them, The harvest truly *is* great, but the labourers *are* few : pray ye therefore the Lord of the harvest, tnat He would send forth labourers into His harvest.

Go your ways : behold, I send you forth as lambs among wolves.

Carry neither purse, nor scrip, nor shoes : and salute no man by the way.

And into whatsoever house ye enter, first say Peace *be* to this house.

And if the son of peace be there, your peace shall rest upon it : if not, it shall turn to you again.

And in the same house remain, eating and drinking such things as they give : for the labourer is worthy of his hire. Go not from house to house.

And into whatsoever city ye enter, and they receive you, eat such things as are set before you :

And heal the sick that are therein, and say unto them, The kingdom of God is come nigh unto you.

But into whatsoever city ye enter, and they receive you not, go your ways out into the streets of the same, and say,

Even the very dust of your city, which cleaveth on us, we do wipe off against you : notwithstanding, be ye sure of this, that the kingdom of God is come nigh unto you.

But I say unto you, that it shall be more tolerable in that day for Sodom than for that city.

Woe unto thee, Chorazin, woe unto thee, Bethsaida! for if the mighty works had been done in Tyre and Sidon which have been done in you, they had a great while ago repented, sitting in sackcloth and ashes,

But it shall be more tolerable for Tyre and Sidon at the judgment than for you.

And thou, Capernaum, which art exalted to heaven, shalt be thrust down to hell.

He that heareth you heareth me; he that despiseth you despiseth me; and he that despiseth me despiseth Him that sent me.

¶ And the seventy returned again with joy, saying, Lord, even the devils are subject unto us through thy name.

And He said unto them, I beheld Satan as lightning fall from heaven.

Behold, I give unto you power to tread on serpents and scorpions, and over all the power of the enemy; and nothing shall by any means hurt you.

Notwithstanding, in this rejoice not, that the spirits are subject unto you; but rather rejoice because your names are written in heaven.

¶ In that hour Jesus rejoiced in spirit, and said, I thank thee, O Father, Lord of heaven and earth, that thou hast hid these things from the wise and prudent, and hast revealed them unto babes: even so, Father; for so it seemed good in thy sight.

All things are delivered

to me of my Father: and no man knoweth who the Son is, but the Father; and who the Father is, but the Son, and *he* to whom the Son will reveal *Him*.

¶ And He turned Him unto *his* disciples, and said privately, Blessed *are* the eyes which see the things that ye see:

For I tell you, that many prophets and kings have desired to see those things which ye see, and have not seen *them;* and to hear those things which ye hear, and have not heard *them*

Now the Jews' feast of tabernacles was at hand.

His brethren therefore said unto Him, Depart hence, and go into Judea, that thy disciples also may see the works that thou doest.

For *there is* no man *that* doeth any thing in secret, and he himself seeketh to be known openly. If thou do these things, shew thyself to the world.

For neither did His brethren believe in Him.

Then Jesus said unto them My time is not yet come: but your time is always ready.

The world cannot hate you; but me it hateth, because I testify of it, that the works thereof are evil.

Go ye up unto this feast: I go not up yet unto this feast; for my time is not yet full come.

When He had said these words unto them, he abode *still* in Galilee.

¶ And it came to pass, when the time was come that He should be received up, He steadfastly set His face to go to Jerusalem,

And sent messengers before His face: and they

went, and entered into a village of the Samaritans, to make ready for Him,

And they did not receive Him, because His face was as though He would go to Jerusalem.

And when His disciples James and John saw *this* they said, Lord, wilt thou that we command fire to come down from heaven, and consume them, even as Elias did?

But He turned, and rebuked them, and said, Ye know not what manner of spirit ye are of.

For the Son of Man is not come to destroy men's lives, but to save *them*. And they went to another village.

CHRIST HEALETH THE LEPERS.

And as He entered into a certain village, there met Him ten men that were lepers, which stood afar off:

And they lifted up *their* voices, and said, Jesus, Master, have mercy on us.

And when He saw *them*, He said unto them, Go shew yourselves unto the priests. And it came to pass, that, as they went, they were cleansed.

And one of them, when he saw that he was healed, turned back, and with a loud voice glorified God,

And fell down on *his* face at His feet, giving Him thanks: and he was a Samaritan.

And Jesus answering said, Were there not ten cleansed, but where *are* the nine?

There are not found that returned to give glory to God, save this stranger.

And He said unto him, Arise, go thy way: thy

faith hath made thee whole.

CHRIST TEACHETH THE LAWYER.

And behold, a certain lawyer stood up and tempted Him, saying, Master, what shall I do to inherit eternal life?

He said unto him, What is written in the law? how readest thou?

And he answering said, Thou shalt love the Lord thy God with all thy heart, and with all thy soul, and with all thy strength, and with all thy mind; and thy neighbour as thyself.

And He said unto him, Thou hast answered right: This do, and thou shalt live.

But he, willing to justify himself, said unto Jesus, And who is my neighbour?

And Jesus answering said, A certain *man* went down from Jerusalem to Jericho, and fell among thieves, which stripped him of his raiment, and wounded *him*, and departed, leaving *him* half dead.

And by chance there came down a certain priest that way; and when he saw him, he passed by on the other side.

And likewise a Levite, when he was at the place, came and looked *on him*, and passed by on the other side.

But a certain Samaritan, as he journeyed, came where he was; and when he saw him, he had compassion *on him*,

And went to *him*, and bound up his wounds, pouring in oil and wine, and set him on his own beast, and brought him to an inn, and took care of him.

And on the morrow when he departed, he took out

two pence, and gave *them* to the host, and said unto him, Take care of him: and whatsoever thou spendest more, when I come again I will repay thee.

Which now of these three, thinkest thou, was neighbour unto him that fell among the theives?

And he said, He that shewed mercy on him. Then said Jesus unto him, Go, and do thou likewise.

AND it came to pass, that, as He was praying in a certain place, when He ceased one of His disciples said unto Him, Lord, teach us to pray, as John also taught his disciples.

And He said unto them, When ye pray say, Our Father which art in heaven, Hallowed be thy name. Thy kingdom come, Thy will be done, as in heaven, so in earth.

Give us day by day our daily bread.

And forgive us our sins; for we also forgive every one that is indebted to us. And lead us not into temptation; but deliver us from evil.

And He said unto them, Which of you shall have a friend, and shall go unto him at midnight, and say unto him, Friend, lend me three loaves;

For a friend of mine in his journey is come to me, and I have nothing to set before him?

And he from within shall answer and say, Trouble me not: the door is now shut, and my children are with me in bed; I cannot rise and give thee.

I say unto you, Though he will not rise and give him, because he is his friend, yet because of his importunity, he will rise

"Take care of him: and whatsoever thou spendest more, when I come again I will repay thee."

and give him as many as he needeth.

And I say unto you, Ask, and it shall be given unto you; seek, and ye shall find; knock, and it shall be opened unto you.

For every one that asketh receiveth; and he that seeketh findeth; and to him that knocketh it shall be opened.

If a son shall ask bread of any of you that is a father, will he give him a stone? or if *he ask* a fish, will he for a fish give him a serpent?

Or if he shall ask an egg, will he offer him a scorpion?

If ye then, being evil, know how to give good gifts unto your children; how much more shall *your* heavenly Father give the Holy Spirit to them that ask Him?

MARTHA AND MARY

Now it came to pass, as they went, that He entered into a certain village: and a certain woman named Martha received Him into her house.

And she had a sister called Mary, which also sat at Jesus' feet, and heard His word.

But Martha was cumbered about much serving, and came to Him, and said, Lord, dost thou not care that my sister hath left me to serve alone? bid her therefore that she help me.

And Jesus answered and said unto her, Martha, Martha, thou art careful and troubled about many things:

But one thing is needful; and Mary hath chosen that good part, which shall not be taken away from her.

THE JEWS FEAST OF TABER-
NACLES AT JERUSALEM.

THE Jews sought Him at the feast, and said, Where is He?

And there was much murmuring among the people concerning Him: for some said, He is a good man: others said, Nay; but He deceiveth the people.

Howbeit no man spake openly of Him for fear of the Jews.

¶ Now about the midst of the feast Jesus went up into the temple, and taught.

And the Jews marvelled, saying, How knoweth this man letters, having never learned?

Jesus answered them and said, My doctrine is not mine, but His that sent me.

If any man will do His will, he shall know of the doctrine, whether it be of God, or *whether* I speak of myself.

He that speaketh of himself seeketh his own glory: but He that seeketh His glory that sent Him, the same is true, and no unrighteousness is in Him.

Did not Moses give you the law, and *yet* none of you keepeth the law? Why go ye about to kill me?

The people answered and said, Thou hast a devil: who goeth about to kill thee?

Jesus answered and said unto them, I have done one work, and ye all marvel.

Moses therefore gave unto you circumcision; (not because it is of Moses, but of the fathers;) and ye on the sabbath day circumcise a man.

If a man on the sabbath day receive circumcision, that the law of Moses should not be broken; are

"Mary hath chosen that good part which shall not be taken away from her."

ye angry at me, because I have made a man every whit whole on the sabbath day?

Judge not according to the appearance, but judge righteous judgment.

Then said some of them of Jerusalem, Is not this He, whom they seek to kill?

But, lo, He speaketh boldly, and they say nothing unto Him. Do the rulers know indeed that this is the very Christ?

Howbeit we know this man whence he is: but when Christ cometh, no man knoweth whence He is.

Then cried Jesus in the temple as He taught, saying, Ye both know me, and ye know whence I am: and I am not come of myself, but He that sent me is true, whom ye know not.

But I know Him; for I am from Him, and He hath sent me.

Then they sought to take Him: but no man laid hands on Him, because His hour was not yet come.

And many of the people believed on Him and said, When Christ cometh, will He do more miracles than these which this *man* hath done?

¶ The Pharisees heard that the people murmured such things concerning Him; and the Pharisees and the chief priests sent officers to take Him.

Then said Jesus unto them, Yet a little while am I with you, and *then* I go unto Him that sent me.

Ye shall seek me, and shall not find *me :* and where I am, *thither* ye cannot come.

Then said the Jews among themselves, Whither will He go, that we shall not find Him? will he go unto the dispersed among the Gentiles, and teach the Gentiles?

What *manner* of saying is this that He said, Ye shall seek me, and shall not find *me:* and where I am, *thither* ye cannot come.

In the last day, that great *day* of the feast, Jesus stood and cried, saying, If any man thirst, let him come unto me and drink.

He that believeth on me, as the Scripture hath said, out of his belly shall flow rivers of living water.

(But this spake He of the Spirit, which they that believe on Him should receive: for the Holy Ghost was not yet *given;* because that Jesus was not yet glorified.)

¶ Many of the people therefore, when they heard this saying, said, Of a truth this is the Prophet.

Others said, This is the Christ. But some said, Shall Christ come out of Galilee?

Hath not the Scripture said, That Christ cometh of the seed of David, and out of the town of Bethlehem, where David was?

So there was a division among the people because of Him.

And some of them would have taken Him; but no man laid hands on Him.

¶ Then came the officers to the chief priests and Pharisees; and they said unto them, Why have ye not brought Him?

The officers answered, Never man spake like this man.

Then answered them the Pharisees, Are ye also deceived?

Have any of the rulers or of the Pharisees believed on Him?

But this p e o p l e who
k n o w e t h not the law are
cursed.

Nicodemus s a i t h unto
them, (he that came to Jesus by night, being one of
them,)

Doth our law judge *any*
man before it hear him, and
know what he doeth?

They answered and said
unto him, Art thou also of
Galilee? Search and look:
for out of Galilee ariseth no
prophet.

And every man went unto
his own house.

CHAPTER XXV.

CHRIST DELIVERETH THE
WOMAN TAKEN IN ADULTERY.

JESUS went unto t h e
mount of Olives.

And early in the morning
He came again into the
temple, and all the people
came unto Him; and He
sat down, and taught them.

And the s c r i b e s and
Pharisees b r o u g h t unto
Him a woman taken in
adultery; and when they had
set her in the midst,

They said unto H i m ,
Master, this woman was
taken in adultery, in the
very act.

Now Moses in the law
commanded us, that such
should be stoned: but what
sayest thou?

This they said, tempting
Him, that they might have
to accuse Him. But Jesus
stooped down, and with *his*
finger wrote on the ground,
*as though He heard them
not.*

So when they continued
asking Him, He lifted up
Himself, and said unto them,
He that is w i t h o u t sin
among you, let him first
cast a stone at her.

And again He stooped

down, and wrote on the ground.

And they which heard *it,* being convicted by *their own* conscience, went out one by one, beginning at the eldest, *even* unto the last : and Jesus was left alone, and the woman standing in the midst.

When Jesus had lifted up Himself and saw none but the woman, He said unto her, Women, where are those thine accusers? hath no man condemned thee?

She said, No man, Lord. And Jesus said unto her, Neither do I condemn thee: go, and sin no more.

THE LIGHT OF THE WORLD.

THEN spake Jesus again unto them, saying, I am the light of the world : he that followeth me shall not walk in darkness, but shall have the light of life.

The Pharisees therefore said unto Him, Thou bearest record of thyself ; thy record is not true.

Jesus answered and said unto them, Though I bear record of myself, *yet* my record is true : for I know whence I came and whither I go; but ye cannot tell whence I come and whither I go.

Ye judge after the flesh ; I judge no man.

And yet if I judge, my judgment is true : for I am not alone, but I and the Father that sent me.

It is also written in your law, that the testimony of two men is true.

I am one that beareth witness of myself, and the Father that sent me beareth witness of me.

Then said they unto Him, Where is thy Father? Jesus answered, Ye neither know me nor my Father : if ye had known me, ye should

"Neither do I condemn thee; go and sin no more."

have known my Father also.

These words spake Jesus in the treasury, as He taught in the temple: and no man laid hands on Him; for His hour was not yet come.

Then said Jesus again unto them, I go my way, and ye shall seek me, and shall die in your sins: whither I go, ye cannot come.

Then said the Jews, Will He kill himself? because He saith, Whither I go, ye cannot come.

And He said unto them, Ye are from beneath; I am from above: ye are from this world; I am not of this world.

I said therefore unto you, that ye shall die in your sins: for if ye believe not that I am *He*, ye shall die in your sins.

Then said they unto Him, Who art thou? And Jesus saith unto them, Even *the same* that I said unto you from the beginning.

I have many things to say and to judge of you: but He that sent me is true; and I speak to the world those things which I have heard of Him.

They understood not that He spake to them of the Father.

Then said Jesus unto them, When ye have lifted up the Son of Man, then shall ye know that I am *He*, and *that* I do nothing of myself; but as my Father hath taught me, I speak these things.

And He that sent me is with me: the Father hath not left me alone; for I do always those things that please Him.

As He spake these words, many believed on Him.

Then said Jesus to those Jews which believed on

Him, If ye continue in my word, *then* are ye my disciples indeed;

And ye shall know the truth, and the truth shall make you free.

¶ They answered Him, We be Abraham's seed, and were never in bondage to any man: how sayest thou, Ye shall be m a d e free?

Jesus answered t h e m, Verily, verily, I say unto you, Whosoever commiteth sin is the servant of sin.

And the servant abideth not in the house for ever: *but* the Son abideth ever.

If the Son therefore shall make you free, ye shall be free indeed.

I k n o w that ye a r e Abraham's seed; but ye seek to kill me, because my word hath no place in you.

I speak that which I have seen with my Father: and ye do that which ye **have** seen with your father.

They answered and said unto Him, Abraham is our father. Jesus saith unto them, If ye were Abraham's children, ye would do the works of Abraham.

But now ye seek to kill me, a man that hath told you the truth, which I have heard of God: this did not Abraham.

Ye do the deeds of your father. Then said they to Him, We be not born of fornication; we have one Father, *even* God.

Jesus said unto them, If God were your Father, ye would love me: for I proceeded forth and came from God; neither came I of myself, but He sent me.

Why do ye not understand my speech? *even* because ye cannot hear my word.

Ye are of *your* father the

devil, and the lusts of your father ye will do: he was a murderer from the beginning, and abode not in the truth, because there is no truth in him. When he speaketh a lie, he speaketh of his own: for he is a liar, and the father of it.

And because I tell *you* the truth, ye believe me not.

Which of you convinceth me of sin? And if I say the truth, why do ye not believe me?

He that is of God heareth God's words: ye therefore hear *them* not, because ye are not of God.

Then answered the Jews and said unto Him, Say we not well that thou art a Samaritan, and hast a devil?

Jesus answered, I have not a devil; but I honour my Father, and ye do dishonour me.

And I seek not mine own glory: there is one that seeketh and judgeth.

Verily, verily, I say unto you, If a man keep my saying, he shall never see death.

Then said the Jews unto Him, Now we know that thou hast a devil. Abraham is dead and the prophets; and thou sayest, If a man keep my saying, he shall never taste of death.

Art thou greater than our father Abraham, which is dead? and the prophets are dead: whom makest thou thyself?

Jesus answered, If I honour myself, my honour is nothing: it is my Father that honoureth me; of whom ye say, that He is your God;

Yet ye have not known Him; but I know Him: and if I should say, I know Him not, I shall be a liar like unto you : but I know Him, and keep His saying.

Your father Abraham rejoiced to see my day : and he saw *it*, and was glad.

Then said the Jews unto Him, Thou art not yet fifty years old, and hast thou seen Abraham?

Jesus said unto them, Verily, verily, I say unto you, Before Abraham was, I am.

Then took they up stones to cast at Him : but Jesus hid Himself, and went out of the temple, going through the midst of them, and so passed by.

SIGHT GIVEN TO ONE BORN BLIND.

AND as *Jesus* passed by, He saw a man which was blind from *his* birth.

And His disciples asked Him, saying, Master, who did sin, this man, or his parents that, he was born blind.

Jesus answered, Neither hath this man sinned, nor his parents : but that the works of God should be made manifest in him.

I must work the works of Him that sent me, while it is day : the night cometh, when no man can work.

As long as I am in the world, I am the light of the world.

When He had thus spoken, He spat on the ground, and made clay of the spittle, and He ancinted the eyes of the blind man with the clay,

And said unto him, Go, wash in the pool of Siloam, (which is by interpretation, Sent.) He went his way therefore, and washed, and came seeing.

¶ The neighbours therefore, and they which before

"Go, wash in the pool of Siloam."

The pool of Siloam.

had seen him that he was blind, said, Is not this he that sat and begged?

Some said, This is he: others *said*, He is like him: *but* he said, I am *he*.

Therefore said they unto him, How were thine eyes opened?

He answered and said, A man that is called Jesus made clay, and anointed mine eyes, and said unto me, Go to the pool of Siloam, and wash: and I went and washed, and I received sight.

Then said they unto him, Where is He? He said, I know not.

¶ They brought to the Pharisees him that aforetime was blind.

And it was the sabbath day when Jesus made the clay, and opened his eyes.

Then again the Pharisees also asked him how he had received his sight. He said unto them, He put clay upon mine eyes, and I washed, and do see.

Therefore said some of the Pharisees, This man is not of God, because He keepeth not the sabbath day. Others said, How can a man that is a sinner do such miracles? And there was a division among them.

They say unto the blind man again, What sayest thou of Him, that He hath opened thine eyes? He said, He is a prophet.

But the Jews did not believe concerning him, that he had been blind, and received his sight, until they called the parents of him that had received his sight.

And they asked them, saying, Is this your son, who ye say was born blind? how then doth he now see?

His parents answered them and said, We know

that this is our son and that he was born blind :

But by what means he now seeth we know not ; or who hath opened his eyes we know not : he is of age ; ask him : he shall speak for himself.

These *words* spake his parents, because they feared the Jews : for the Jews had agreed already, that if any man did confess He was Christ, he should be put out of the synagogue.

Therefore said his parents, He is of age ; ask him.

Then again called they the man that was blind, and said unto him, Give God the praise : we know that this man is a sinner.

He answered and said, Whether He be a sinner *or no*, I know not : one thing I know, that whereas I was blind, now I see.

Then said they to him again, What did He to thee? how opened He thine eyes?

He answered them, I have told you already, and ye did not hear : wherefore would you hear *it* again? will ye also be His disciples?

Then they reviled him, and said, Thou art His disciple ; but we are Moses' disciples.

We know that God spake unto Moses : *as for* this *fellow*, we know not from whence He is.

The man answered and said unto them, Why herein is a marvellous thing, that ye know not from whence He is, and *yet* He hath opened mine eyes.

Now we know that God heareth not sinners : but if any man be a worshipper of God and doeth His will, him He heareth.

Since the world began was it not heard that any

man opened the eyes of one that was born blind.

If this man were not of God, He could do nothing.

They answered and said unto him, Thou wast altogether born in sins, and dost thou teach us? And they cast him out.

Jesus heard that they had cast him out ; and when He had found him, He said unto him, Dost thou believe on the Son of God?

He answered and said, Who is He, Lord, that I might believe on Him?

And Jesus said unto him, Thou hast both seen Him, and it is He that talketh with thee.

And he said, Lord, I believe. And he worshipped Him.

¶ And Jesus said, For judgment I am come into this world, that they which see not might see ; and that they which see might be made blind.

And *some* of the Pharisees which were with Him heard these words, and said unto Him, Are we blind also :

Jesus said unto them, If ye were blind, ye should have no sin : but now ye say, We see ; therefore your sin remaineth.

CHAPTER XXVI.

CHRIST, THE GOOD SHEPHERD.

VERILY, verily, I say unto you, He that entereth not by the door into the sheepfold, but climbeth up some other way, the same is a thief and a robber.

But he that entereth in by the door is the shepherd of the sheep.

To him the porter openeth ; and the sheep hear

his voice: and he calleth his own sheep by name, and leadeth them out.

And when he putteth forth his own sheep, he goeth before them, and the sheep follow him: for they know his voice.

And a stranger will they not follow, but will flee from him: for they know not the voice of strangers.

This parable spake Jesus unto them; but they understood not what things they were which He spake unto them.

Then said Jesus unto them again, Verily, verily, I say unto you, I am the door of the sheep.

All that ever came before me are thieves and robbers: but the sheep did not hear them.

I am the door: by me if any man enter in, he shall be saved, and shall go in and out, and find pasture.

The thief cometh not, but for to steal, and to kill, and to destroy; I am come that they might have life, and that they might have *it* more abundantly.

I am the good shepherd: the good shepherd giveth his life for the sheep.

But he that is a hireling, and not the shepherd, whose own the sheep are not, seeth the wolf coming, and leaveth the sheep, and fleeth; and the wolf catcheth them, and scattereth the sheep.

The hireling fleeth, because he is a hireling, and careth not for the sheep.

I am the good shepherd, and know my *sheep*, and am known of mine.

As the Father knoweth me, even so know I the Father: and I lay down my life for the sheep.

And other sheep I have, which are not of this fold:

them also I must bring, and they shall hear my voice; and there shall be one fold, *and* one shepherd.

Therefore doth my Father love me, because I lay down my life, that I might take it again.

No man taketh it from me, but I lay it down of myself. I have power to lay it down, and I have power to take it again. This commandment have I received of my father.

¶ There was a division therefore again among the Jews for these sayings.

And many of them said, He hath a devil and is mad; why hear ye Him?

Others said, These are not the words of Him that hath a devil. Can a devil open the eyes of the blind?

¶ And it was at Jerusalem the feast of the dedication, and it was winter.

And Jesus walked in the temple in Solomon's porch.

Then came the Jews round about Him, and said unto Him, How long dost thou make us to doubt? If thou be the Christ, tell us plainly.

Jesus answered them, I told you and ye believed not: the works that I do in my Father's name, they bear witness of me.

But ye believe not, because ye are not of my sheep as I said unto you.

My sheep hear my voice, and I know them, and they follow me:

And I give unto them eternal life; and they shall never perish, neither shall any *man* pluck them out of my hand.

My Father, which gave *them* me, is greater than all; and no *man* is able to pluck *them* out of my Father's hand.

I and *my* Father are one.

Then the Jews took up stones again to stone Him.

Jesus answered them, Many good works have I shewed you from my Father; for which of those works do ye stone me?

The Jews answered Him, saying, For a good work we stone thee not; but for blasphemy; and because that thou, being a man, makest thyself God.

Jesus answered them, Is it not written in your law, I said, Ye are gods?

If he called them gods, unto whom the word of God came, and the Scripture cannot be broken;

Say ye of Him, whom the Father hath sanctified, and sent into the world, Thou blasphemest; because I said, I am the Son of God?

If I do not the works of my Father, believe me not.

But if I do, though ye believe not me, believe the works; that ye may know, and believe, that the Father *is* in me, and I in Him.

Therefore they sought again to take Him; but He escaped out of their hand,

And went away again beyond Jordan into the place where John at first baptized; and there He abode.

And many resorted unto Him and said, John did no miracle: but all things that John spake of this man were true.

And great multitudes followed Him; and He healed them, and, as He was wont, He taught them.

And many believed on Him there.

¶ The Pharisees also came unto Him, tempting Him, and saying unto Him, Is it lawful for a man to

THE LAW.

put away his wife for every cause?

And He answered and said unto them, Have ye not read that He which made *them* at the beginning made t h e m male a n d female,

And said, For this cause shall a man leave father and mother, and shall cleave to his wife: and they twain shall be one flesh?

Wherefore they are no more twain, but one flesh. What therefore God has joined together let no man put asunder.

They say unto Him, Why did Moses then command to give a writing of divorcement and to put her away.

He saith unto them, Moses because of the hardness of your hearts suffered you to put away your wives: but from the beginning it was not so.

And I say unto you, Whosoever shall put away his wife, except *it be* for fornication, and shall marry another, committeth adultery: and whoso marrieth her which is put away doth commit adultery.

¶ His disciples say unto Him, If the case of the man be so with *his* wife, it is not good to marry.

But He said unto them, All *men* cannot receive this saying, save *they* to whom it is given.

For there are some eunuchs, which were so born from *their* mother's womb: and there are some eunuchs, which were made eunuchs of men: and there be eunuchs, which h a v e made themselves eunuchs for the kingdom of heaven's sake. He that is able to receive *it*, let him receive *it*.

CHAPTER XXVII

CHILDREN BROUGHT TO CHRIST

THEN were there brought unto Him little children, that He should put *His* hands on them, and pray : and the disciples rebuked them.

But when Jesus saw *it*, He was much displeased, and called them unto Him, and said, Suffer the little children to come unto me, and forbid them not: for of such is the kingdom of heaven.

Verily I say unto you, Whosoever shall not receive the kingdom of God as a little child, he shall not enter therein.

And He took them up in His arms, put *His* hands upon them and blessed them.

And when He was gone forth into the way, there came a certain ruler and kneeled to Him, saying, Good master, what good thing shall I do, that I may have eternal life?

And Jesus said unto him, Why callest thou me good? *there is* none good but one, *that is*, God : but if thou wilt enter into life, keep the commandments.

He saith unto Him, Which? Jesus said, Thou shalt do no murder, Thou shalt not commit adultery, Thou shalt not steal, Thou shalt not bear false witness,

Honour thy father and *thy* mother : and, Thou shalt love thy neighbour as thyself.

The young man saith unto Him, Master, all these have I kept from my youth up : what lack I yet?

Then Jesus, beholding him, loved him, and said unto him, One thing thou lackest : If thou wilt be

"Suffer the little children to come unto Me, and forbid them not: for of such is the kingdom of heaven."

perfect, go thy way, sell whatsoever thou hast, and give to the poor, and thou shalt have treasure in heaven: and come, take up the cross, and follow me.

But when the young man heard that saying, he was sad, and went away sorrowful: for he had great possessions.

And when Jesus saw that he was very sorrowful, he looked round about, and saith unto His disciples, How hardly shall they that have riches enter into the kingdom of God!

Verily I say unto you, That a rich man shall hardly enter into the kingdom of heaven.

And the disciples were astonished at His words. But Jesus answereth again, and saith unto them, Children, how hard is it for them that trust in riches to enter into the kingdom of God!

It is easier for a camel to go through the eye of a needle, than for a rich man to enter into the kingdom of God,

When His disciples heard *it*, they were exceedingly amazed, and astonished out of measure, saying among themselves, Who then can be saved?

And Jesus, looking upon them, saith, With men this is impossible; but the things which are impossible with men are possible with God, for with God all things are possible.

Then answered Peter and said unto Him, Behold, we have forsaken all, and followed thee; what shall we have therefore?

And Jesus said unto them, Verily I say unto you, That ye which have followed me, in the regeneration when the Son of Man shall sit in the throne of His glory, ye also shall sit upon twelve thrones, judging the twelve tribes of Israel.

And every one that hath forsaken houses, or brethern or sisters, or f a t h e r , or mother, or wife, or children, or lands, for my name's sake, and the gospel's shall receive an hundredfold now in this time, houses, and brethren, and sisters, and mothers, and children, and lands, w i t h persecutions ; and in the world to come, eternal life.

But many *that are* first shall be last ; and the last first.

For the k i n g d o m of heaven is like unto a man *that is* an householder, which went out early in the morning to hire labourers into his vineyard.

And when he had agreed with the labourers for a penny a day, he sent them into his vineyard.

And he went out about the third hour, and saw others standing i d l e in the marketplace, and said unto them : Go ye also into the vineyard, and whatsoever is right I will give you. And they went their way.

Again he went out about the sixth and ninth hour, and did likewise.

And about the eleventh hour he went out, and found others standing idle, and saith unto them, Why stand ye here all the day idle ?

They say unto him, Because no man hath hired us. He saith unto them, Go ye also into the vineyard : and whatsoever is right, *that* shall ye receive.

So when even was come, the lord of the vineyard saith unto his steward, Call the labourers, and give them *their* hire, beginning from the last unto the first.

And when they came that *were hired* about the eleventh hour, they received every man a penny.

But when the first came, they supposed that they should have received more; and they likewise received every man a penny.

And when they had received *it*, they murmured against the goodman of the house, saying, These last have wrought *but* one hour, and thou hast made them equal unto us, which have borne the burden and heat of the day.

But he answered one of them, and said, Friend, I do thee no wrong: didst not thou agree with me for a penny?

Take *that* thine *is*, and go thy way: I will give unto this last even as unto thee. Is it not lawful for me to do what I will with mine own? Is thine eye evil, because I am good:

So the last shall be first, and the first last: for many be called, but few chosen.

¶ And He was teaching in one of the synagogues on the sabbath.

And behold, there was a woman which had a spirit of infirmity eighteen years, and was bowed together, and could in no wise lift up *herself*.

And when Jesus saw her, He called *her to Him*, and said unto her, Woman, thou art loosed from thine infirmity. And He laid *His* hands on her: and immediately she was made straight, and glorified God.

And the ruler of the synagogue answered with indignation, because that Jesus had healed on the sabbath day: and said unto the people, There are six days in which men ought to work: in them therefore come and be healed, and not on the sabbath day.

The Lord then answered him, and said, *Thou* hypocrite, doth not each one of you on the sabbath loose his ox or *his* ass from the stall, and lead *him* away to watering?

And ought not this woman, being a daughter of Abraham, whom Satan hath bound, lo, these eighteen years, be loosed from this bond on the sabbath day?

And when He had said these things, all His adversaries were ashamed: and all the people rejoiced for all the glorious things that were done by Him.

Then said He, unto what is the kingdom of God like? and whereunto shall I resemble it?

It is like a grain of mustard seed, which a man took, and cast into his garden; and it grew and waxed a great tree; and the fowls of the air lodged in the branches of it.

And again He said, Whereunto shall I liken the kingdom of God?

It is like leaven, which a woman took and hid in three measures of meal, till the whole was leavened.

Then said one unto Him, Lord, are there few that be saved? And He said unto them,

Strive to enter in at the straight gate: for many I say unto you, will seek to enter in, and shall not be able.

When once the master of the house is risen up and hath shut to the door, and ye begin to stand without, and to knock at the door, saying, Lord, Lord, open unto us; and He shall answer and say unto you, I know you not whence ye are.

Then shall ye begin to say, We have eaten and drunk in thy presence, and thou hast taught in our streets.

But He shall say, I tell you, I know you not whence ye are; depart from me, all ye workers of iniquity.

There shall be weeping and gnashing of teeth when ye shall see Abraham, and Isaac, and Jacob, and all the prophets, in the kingdom of God, and you *yourselves* thrust out.

And they shall come from the east, and *from* the west; and from the north, and *from* the south, and shall sit down in the kingdom of God.

And behold, there are last which shall be first; and there are first which shall be last.

The same day there came certain of the Pharisees, saying unto Him, Get thee out and depart hence; for Herod will kill thee.

And He said unto them, Go ye and tell that fox, Behold, I cast out devils, and I do cures to-day and to-morrow, and the third *day* I shall be perfected.

Nevertheless I must walk to-day and to-morrow, and the *day* following: for it cannot be that a prophet perish out of Jerusalem.

O Jerusalem, Jerusalem, which killest the prophets, and stonest them that are sent unto thee; how often would I have gathered thy children together as a hen *doth gather* her brood under *her* wings, and ye would not!

Behold, your house is left unto you desolate: and verily I say unto you, Ye shall not see me until *the time* come when ye shall say, Blessed *is* He that cometh in the name of the Lord.

CHAPTER XXVIII.

CHRIST HEALETH THE DROPSY.

AND it came to pass, as He went into the house of one of the chief Pharisees to eat bread on the sabbath day, that they watched Him.

And behold, there was a certain man before Him which had the dropsy.

And Jesus answering spake unto the lawyers and Pharisees, saying, Is it lawful to heal on the sabbath day?

And they held their peace. And He took *him*, and healed him, and let him go;

And answered them, saying, Which of you shall have an ass or an ox fallen into a pit, and will not straightway pull him out on the sabbath day?

And they could not answer Him again to these things.

And He put forth a parable to those which were bidden, when He marked how they chose out the chief rooms; saying unto them,

When thou art bidden of any *man* to a wedding, sit not down in the highest rooms; lest a more honorable man than thou be bidden of him;

And he that bade thee and him, come and say to thee, Give this man place; and thou begin with shame to take the lowest room.

But when thou art bidden, go and sit down in the lowest room; that when he that bade thee, cometh, he may say unto thee, Friend, go up higher: then shalt thou have worship in the pres-

And they held their peace. And He took *him*, and healed him, and let him go.

ence of them that sit at meat with thee.

For whosoever exalteth himself shall be abased; and he that humbleth himself shall be exalted.

Then said He also to him that bade Him, When thou makest a dinner or a supper call not thy friends, nor thy brethren, neither thy kinsmen, nor *thy* rich neighbonrs; lest they also bid thee again, and a recompense be made thee.

But when thou makest a feast, call the poor, the maimed, the blind: and thou shalt be blessed; for they cannot recompense thee: for thou shalt be recompensed at the resurrection of the just.

And when one of them that sat at meat with Him heard these things, he said unto Him, Blessed *is* he that shall eat bread in the kingdom of God!

Then said He unto him, A certain man made a great supper and bade many: and sent his servant at supper time, to say to them that were bidden, Come: for all things are now ready.

And they all with one *consent*, began to make excuse. The first said unto him, I have bought a piece of ground, and I must needs go and see it: I pray thee have me excused.

And another said, I have bought five yoke of oxen, and I go to prove them: I pray thee have me excused.

And another said, I have married a wife, and therefore I cannot come.

So that servant came and shewed his lord these things. Then the master of the house, being angry, said to his servant, Go out quickly into the streets and lanes of the city, and bring in hither the poor, and the maimed, and the halt, and the blind.

And the servant said, Lord, it is done as thou hast commanded, and yet there is room.

And the lord said unto the servant, Go out into the highways and hedges, and compel *them* to come in, that my house may be filled. For I say unto you, That none of those men which were bidden, shall taste of my supper.

HIS DISCIPLES TO BEAR THEIR CROSS.

AND there went great multitudes with Him: and He turned, and said unto them.

If any man *come* to me and hate not his father and mother, and wife, and children, and brethren, and sisters, yea, and his own life also, cannot be my disciple.

And whosoever doth not bear his cross, and come after me, cannot be my disciple.

For which of you, intending to build a tower, sitteth not down first, and counteth the cost, whether he have *sufficient* to finish *it?*

Lest haply, after he hath laid the foundation, and is not able to finish *it*, all that behold *it*, begin to mock him, saying, This man began to build, and was not able to finish.

Or what king, going to make war against another king, sitteth not down first, and consulteth whether he be able with ten thousand, to meet him that cometh against him with twenty thousand?

Or else, while the other is yet a great way off, he sendeth an ambassage, and desireth conditions of peace.

So likewise, whosoever he be of you that forsaketh

And not many days after, the younger son gathered all together, and took his journey into a far country.

not all that he hath, he cannot be my disciple.

Salt *is* good : but if the salt have lost his savour, wherewith shall it be seasoned.

It is neither fit for the land, nor yet for the dunghill ; *but* men cast it out. He that hath ears to hear, let him hear.

THE PRODIGAL SON.

Then drew near unto Him all the publicans and sinners to hear Him.

And the Pharisees and scribes murmured, saying, This man receiveth sinners, and eateth with them.

And He spake this parable unto them, saying,

What man of you, having a hundred sheep, if he lose one of them, doth not leave the ninety and nine in the wilderness, and go after that which is lost, until he find it ?

And when he hath found *it*, he layeth *it* on his shoulders, rejoicing.

And when he cometh home, he calleth together *his* friends and neighbors, saying unto them, Rejoice with me ; for I have found my sheep which was lost.

I say unto you, that likewise joy shall be in heaven over one sinner that repenteth, more than over ninety and nine just persons, which need no repentance.

Either what woman having ten pieces of silver, if she lose one piece, doth not light a candle, and sweep the house, and s e e k diligently till she find *it ?*

And when she hath found *it*, she calleth *her* friends and *her* neighbours together, saying, Rejoice with me ; for I have found the piece which I had lost.

Likewise, I say unto you,

there is joy in the presence of the angels of God over one sinner that repenteth.

And He said, a certain man had two sons:

And the younger of them said to *his* father, Father, give me the portion of goods that falleth *to me*. And he divided unto them *his* living.

And not many days after, the younger son gathered all together, and took his journey into a far country, and there wasted his substance with riotous living.

And when he had spent all, there arose a mighty famine in that land; and he began to be in want.

And he went and joined himself to a citizen of that country; and he sent him into his fields to feed swine.

And he would fain have filled his belly with the husks that the swine did eat: and no man gave unto him.

And when he came to himself, he said. How many hired servants of my father's have bread enough and to spare, and I perish with hunger!

I will arise and go to my father, and will say unto him, Father, I have sinned against heaven, and before thee, and am no more worthy to be called thy son: make me as one of thy hired servants.

And he arose, and came to his father. But when he was yet a great way off, his father saw him, and had compassion, and ran, and fell on his neck, and kissed him.

And the son said unto him, Father, I have sinned against heaven, and in thy sight, and am no more worthy to be called thy son.

But the father said to his servants, Bring forth the best robe, and put *it* on

And he arose, and came to his father.

him; and put a ring on his hand, and shoes on *his* feet:

And bring hither the fatted calf, and kill *it;* and let us eat, and be merry: for this my son was dead, and is alive again; he was lost, and is found! And they began to be merry.

Now the elder son was in the field: and as he came and drew nigh to the house, he heard music and dancing.

And he called one of the servants, and asked what these things meant.

And he said unto him, Thy brother is come; and thy father hath killed the fatted calf, because he hath received him safe and sound.

And he was angry, and would not go in: therefore came his father out, and entreated him.

And he answering said to *his* father, Lo, these many years do I serve thee, neither transgressed I at any time thy commandment; and yet thou never gavest me a kid, that I might make merry with my friends:

But as soon as this thy son was come, which hath devoured thy living with harlots, thou hast killed for him the fatted calf.

And he said unto him, Son, thou art ever with me, and all that I have is thine.

It was meet that we should make merry and be glad: for this thy brother was dead, and is alive again; and was lost and is found!

CHAPTER XXIX.

PARABLE OF THE UNJUST STEWARD.

AND He said also unto His disciples, There was a certain rich man, which had a steward? and the same was accused unto him that he had wasted his goods.

And he called him and said unto him, How is it that I hear this of thee; give an account of thy stewardship; for thou mayest be no longer steward.

Then the steward said within himself, What shall I do? for my lord taketh away from me the stewardship; I cannot dig; to beg I am ashamed.

I am resolved what to do, that, when I am put out of the stewardship, they may receive me into their houses.

So he called every one of his lord's debtors *unto him*, and said unto the first, How much owest thou my lord?

And he said a hundred measures of oil. And he said unto him, Take thy bill, and sit down quickly and write fifty.

Then said he to another, And how much owest thou? And he said a hundred measures of wheat. And he said unto him, Take thy bill and write fourscore.

And the lord commended the unjust steward, because he had done wisely: for the children of this world are in their generation wiser than the children of light.

And I say unto you, Make to yourselves friends of the mammon of unrighteousness; that, when ye fail, they may receive you into everlasting habitations.

He that is faithful in that which is least, is faithful also in much: and he that is unjust in the least, is unjust also in much.

If therefore ye have not been faithful in the unrighteous mammon, who will commit to your trust the true *riches?*

And if ye have not been faithful in that which is another man's, who shall give you that which is your own?

No servant can serve two masters: for either he will hate the one, and love the other ; or else he will hold to the one, and despise the other. Ye cannot serve God and mammon.

And the Pharisees also, who were covetous, heard all these things : and they derided Him.

And He said unto them, Ye are they which justify yourselves before men ; but God knoweth your hearts : for that which is highly esteemed among men, is abomination in the sight of God.

The law and the prophets *were* until John : since that time the kingdom of God is preached, and every man presseth into it.

And it is easier for heaven and earth to pass, than one tittle of the law to fail.

Whosoever putteth away his wife, and marrieth another, committeth adultery: and whosoever marrieth her that is put away from *her* husband, committeth adultery.

THE GLUTTON AND THE BEGGAR.

There was a certain rich man which was clothed in purple and fine linen, and fared sumptuously every day.

And there was a certain beggar named Lazarus, which was laid at his gate, full of sores, and desiring to be fed with the crumbs which fell from the rich man's table. Moreover the dogs came and licked his sores.

And it came to pass, that the beggar died, and was carried by the angels into Abraham's bosom : the rich man also died and was buried.

And in hell he lifted up his eyes, being in torments, and seeth Abraham afar off, and Lazarus in his bosom.

And he cried and said, Father Abraham, have mercy on me, and send Lazarus, that he may dip the tip of his finger in water and cool my tongue, for I am tormented in this flame.

But Abraham said, Son, remember that thou in thy lifetime receivedst thy good things, and likewise Lazarus evil things: but now he is comforted and thou art tormented.

And beside all this, between us and you there is a great gulf fixed: so that they which would pass from hence to you, cannot; neither can they pass to us, that *would come* from thence.

Then he said, I pray thee therefore, father, that thou wouldest send him to my father's house: for I have five brethren; that he may testify unto them, lest they also come into this place of torment.

Abraham said unto him, They have Moses and the prophets; let them hear them.

And he said, Nay, father Abraham: but if one went unto them from the dead, they will repent.

And he said unto him, If they hear not Moses and the prophets, neither will they be persuaded, though one rose from the dead.

¶ Then said He unto the disciples, It is impossible but that offences will come: but woe *unto him*, through whom they come!

It were better for him that a millstone were hanged about his neck, and he cast

And it came to pass, that the beggar died, and was carried by the angels into Abraham's bosom.

into the sea, than that he should offend one of these little ones.

Take heed to yourselves: If thy brother trespass against thee, rebuke him; and if he repent, forgive him.

And if he trespass against thee seven times in a day, and seven times in a day turn again to thee, saying, I repent; thou shalt forgive him.

And the apostles said unto the Lord, Increase our faith.

And the Lord said, If ye had faith as a grain of mustard seed, ye might say unto this sycamine tree, Be thou plucked up by the root, and be thou planted in the sea; and it should obey you.

But which of you, having a servant ploughing or feeding cattle, will say unto him by and by, when he is come from the field, Go and sit down to meat?

And will not rather say unto him, Make ready wherewith I may sup, and gird thyself, and serve me, till I have eaten and drunken; and afterward thou shalt eat and drink?

Doth he thank that servant because he did the things which are commanded him? I trow not.

So likewise ye, when ye shall have done all those things which are commanded you, say, We are unprofitable servants: we have done that which was our duty to do.

THE KINGDOM OF GOD.

AND when He was demanded of the Pharisees, when the kingdom of God should come, He answered them and said, The kingdom of God cometh not with observation: neither shall they say, Lo here ! or, lo there ! for behold, the kingdom of God is within you.

And He said unto the disciples, The days will come when ye shall desire to see one of the days of the Son of man, and ye shall not see *it*.

And they shall say to you, See here ; or, see there, ; go not after *them*, nor follow *them*.

For as the lightning that lighteneth out of the one *part* under heaven, shineth unto the other *part* under heaven ; so shall also the Son of man be in His day.

But first must He suffer many things, and be rejected of this generation.

And as it was in the days of Noe, so shall it be also in the days of the Son of man.

They did eat, they drank, they married wives, they were given in marriage, until the day that Noe entered into the ark, and the flood came, and destroyed them all.

Likewise also as it was in the days of Lot ; they did eat, they d r a n k , they bought, they s o l d , they planted, they builded ;

But the same day that Lot went out of Sodom, it rained fire and brimstone from heaven, and destroyed *them* all.

Even thus shall it be in the day when the Son of man is revealed.

In that day, he which shall be upon the housetop, and his stuff in the house, let him not come down to take it away : and he that is in the field, let him likewise not return back.

Remember Lot's wife !

Whosoever shall seek to save his life shall lose it ;

and whosoever shall lose his life shall preserve it.

I tell you, in that night there shall be two *men* in one bed; the one shall be taken, and the other shall be left.

Two *women* shall be grinding together; the one shall be taken and the other left.

Two *men* shall be in the field; the one shall be taken, and the other left.

And they answered and said unto Him, Where, Lord? And He said unto them, Wheresoever the body *is*, thither will the eagles be gathered together.

OF THE IMPORTUNATE WIDOW.

AND He spake a parable unto them *to this end*, that men ought always to pray, and not to faint.

Saying, There was in a city a judge, which feared not God, neither regarded man.

And there was a widow in that city; and she came unto him, saying, Avenge me of mine adversary.

And he would not for a while, but afterward he said within himself, Though I fear not God, nor regard man; yet because this widow troubleth me, I will avenge her, lest by her continual coming she weary me.

And the Lord said, Hear what the unjust judge saith.

And shall not God avenge His own elect, which cry day and night unto Him, though He bear long with them?

I tell you that He will avenge them speedily. Nevertheless, when the Son of man cometh shall He find faith on the earth?

And He spake this parable unto certain which

trusted in themselves that they were righteous, and despised others.

Two men went up into the temple to pray; the one a Pharisee and the other a publican.

The Pharisee stood up and prayed thus with himself, God, I thank thee, that I am not as other men *are*, extortioners, unjust, adulterers, or even as this publican.

I fast twice in the week, I give tithes of all that I possess.

And the publican, standing afar off, would not lift up so much as *his* eyes unto heaven, but smote upon his breast, saying, God be merciful to me a sinner!

I tell you, this man went down to his house justified *rather* than the other: for every one that exalteth himself shall be abased; and he that **humbleth** himself shall be exalted.

CHAPTER XXX.

CHRIST RAISETH LAZARUS.

NOW a certain *man* was sick, *named* Lazarus, of Bethany, the town of Mary and her sister Martha, (It was *that* Mary which anointed the Lord with ointment, and wiped His feet with her hair, whose brother Lazarus was sick.)

Therefore his sisters sent unto Him, saying, Lord, behold, he whom thou lovest is sick.

When Jesus heard *that* He said, This sickness is not unto death, but for the glory of God, that the Son of God might be glorified thereby.

Now Jesus loved Martha, and her sister, and Lazarus.

When He had heard therefore that he was sick,

He abode two days still in the same place where He was.

Then after that, saith He to *His* disciples, let us go into Judea again.

His disciples say unto Him, Master, the Jews of late sought to stone thee; and goest t h o u thither again?

Jesus answered, Are there not twelve hours in the day? If any man walk in the day, he stumbleth not, because he seeth the light of this world.

But if a man walk in the night, he stumbleth, because there is no light in him.

These things said He: and after that He saith unto them, Our friend Lazarus sleepeth; but I go, that I may awake him out of sleep.

Then said His disciples, Lord, if he sleep, he shall do well.

Howbeit Jesus spake of his death: but they thought that He had spoken of taking rest in sleep.

Then said J e s u s unto them plainly, Lazarus is dead.

And I am glad for your sakes that I was not there, to the intent ye may believe; nevertheless let us go unto him.

Then said Thomas, which is called Didymus, unto his fellow disciples, Let us also go, that we may die with Him.

Then when Jesus came, He found that he had *lain* in the grave four days already.

Now Bethany was nigh unto Jerusalem, about fifteen furlongs off, and many of the Jews came to Martha and Mary, to comfort them concerning their brother.

Then Martha, as soon as she heard that Jesus was

coming, went and met Him: but Mary sat *still* in the house.

Then said Martha unto Jesus, Lord, if thou hadst been here, my brother had not died!

But I know, that even now, whatsoever thou wilt ask of God, God will give *it* thee.

Jesus saith unto her, Thy brother shall rise again.

Martha said unto Him, I know that he shall rise again in the resurrection at the last day.

Jesus said unto her, I am the resurrection and the life: he that believeth in me, though he were dead, yet shall he live: and whosoever liveth and believeth in me shall never die. Believest thou this?

She saith unto Him, Yea, Lord: I believe that Thou art the Christ, the Son of God, which should come into the world.

And when she had so said, she went her way, and called Mary her sister secretly, saying, The Master is come, and calleth for thee.

As soon as she heard *that*, she arose quickly, and came unto Him.

Now Jesus was not yet come into the town, but was in that place where Martha met Him.

The Jews then which were with her in the house, and comforted her, when they saw Mary, that she rose up hastily and went out, followed her, saying, She goeth unto the grave to weep there.

Then when Mary was come where Jesus was, and saw Him, she fell down at His feet, saying unto Him, Lord, if Thou hadst been here, my brother had not died!

And when He had thus spoken, He cried with a loud voice, Lazarus, come forth!

When Jesus therefore saw her weeping, and the Jews also weeping which came with her, He groaned in the spirit, and was troubled;

And said, Where have ye laid him? They said unto Him, Lord, come and see.

Jesus wept.

Then said the Jews, Behold how He loved him!

And some of them said, Could not this man, which opened the eyes of the blind, have caused that even this man should not have died?

Jesus therefore again groaning in Himself cometh to the grave. It was a cave, and a stone lay upon it.

Jesus said, Take ye away the stone. Martha, the sister of him that was dead, saith unto Him, Lord, by this time he stinketh: for he hath been *dead* four days.

Jesus saith unto her, Said I not unto thee, that, if thou wouldest believe, thou shouldest see the glory of God!

Then they took away the stone *from the place* where the dead was laid.

And Jesus lifted up *His* eyes and said, Father, I thank thee that thou hast heard me. And I knew that thou hearest me always; but because of the people which stand by I said *it*, that they may believe that thou hast sent me.

And when He had thus spoken, He cried with a loud voice, Lazarus, come forth!

And he that was dead came forth, bound hand and foot with graveclothes; and his face was bound about with a napkin. Jesus saith unto them, Loose him, and let him go.

Then many of the Jews which came to Mary, and

had seen the things which Jesus did, believed on Him.

But some of them went their ways to the Pharisees, and told them what things Jesus had done.

Then gathered the chief priests and the Pharisees a council, and said, What do we? for this man doeth many miracles.

If we let Him thus alone, all *men* will believe on Him; and the Romans shall come and take away both our place and nation.

And one of them, *named* Caiaphas, being the high priest that same year, said unto them, Ye know nothing at all, nor consider it is expedient for us, that one man should die for the people, and that the whole nation perish not.

And this spake he not of himself: but being high priest that year, he prophesied that Jesus should die for that nation;

And not for that nation only, but that also He should gather together in one the children of God that were scattered abroad.

Then from that day forth they took counsel together to put Him to death.

Jesus therefore walked no more openly among the Jews; but went thence unto a country near to the wilderness, into a city called Ephraim, and there continued with His disciples.

CHAPTER XXXI.

JESUS FORETELLS HIS DEATH AND RESURRECTION.

AND Jesus going up to Jerusalem, took the twelve disciples apart in the way, and began to tell them what things should happen unto Him, saying,

Behold, we go up to Jerusalem; and all things that are written by the prophets concerning the Son of man shall be accomplished.

And they were amazed; and as they followed, they were afraid.

And He said unto them, The Son of man shall be betrayed unto the chief priests and unto the scribes, and they shall condemn Him to death;

And He shall be delivered unto the Gentiles, and shall be mocked, and spitefully entreated, and spitted on:

And they shall scourge *Him*, and put Him to death; and the third day He shall rise again.

And they understood none of these things: and this saying was hid from them, neither knew they the things which were spoken.

¶ Then came to Him the mother of Zebedee's children, with her sons, James and John, worshipping *Him*, and saying, Master, we would that thou shouldest do for us whatsoever we shall desire.

And He said unto them, What would ye that I should do for you?

She said unto Him, Grant that these my two sons may sit, the one on thy right hand and the other on the left, in thy kingdom.

And Jesus answered and said, Ye know not what ye ask. Are ye able to drink of the cup that I shall drink of, and to be baptized with the baptism that I am baptized with? They say unto Him, We are able.

And Jesus said unto them, Ye shall indeed drink of the cup that I drink of; and with the baptism that I am baptized withal shall ye be baptized:

But to sit on my right hand and on my left hand, is not mine to give, but *it shall be given to them* for whom it is prepared of my Father.

And when the ten heard *it*, they were moved with indignation against the two brethren.

But Jesus called them *unto Him*, and said, Ye know that the princes of the Gentiles exercise dominion over them, and they that are great, exercise authority upon them.

But it shall not be so among you: but whosoever will be great among you, let him be your minister; and whosoever will be chief among you, let him be your servant.

For even the Son of man came not to be ministered unto, but to minister, and to give His life a ransom for many.

THE BLIND BEGGAR BARTIMÆUS.

AND it came to pass that as he was come nigh unto Jericho, with His disciples and a great number of people, blind Bartimæus, the the son of Timæus, sat by the highway side begging.

And hearing the multitude pass by, he asked what it meant.

And they told him, that Jesus of Nazareth passeth by

And when he heard that it was Jesus of Nazareth, he began to cry out, and say, Jesus, *thou* Son of David, have mercy on me!

And they which went before, rebuked him; and many charged him that he should hold his peace: but he cried the more a great deal, *thou* Son of David, have mercy on me!

And Jesus answered and said, Ye know not what ye ask.

And Jesus stood still, and commanded him to be called. And they call the blind man, saying unto him, Be of good comfort, rise; He calleth thee!

And he, casting away his garment, rose, and came to Jesus.

And Jesus answered and said unto him, What wilt thou that I should do unto thee? The blind man said unto Him, Lord, that I may receive my sight.

And Jesus said unto him Receive thy sight: thy faith hath saved thee. Go thy way; thy faith hath made thee whole.

And immediately he received his sight, and followed Jesus in the way, glorifying God: and all the people when they saw *it*, gave praise unto God.

OF ZACCHÆUS, A PUBLICAN

AND *Jesus* entered and passed through Jericho.

And behold, *there was* a man named Zacchæus, which was the chief among the publicans, and he was rich.

And he sought to see Jesus who he was; and could not for the press, because he was little of stature.

And he ran before, and climbed up into a sycamore tree to see Him; for He was to pass that *way*.

And when Jesus came to the place, He looked up and saw him, and said unto him, Zacchæus, make haste and come down; for to-day I must abide at thy house.

And he made haste and came down. and received Him joyfully.

And when they saw *it*, They all murmured, saying, That He was gone to be guest with a man that is a sinner.

And Zacchæus stood and said unto the Lord, Behold, Lord, the half of my goods I give to the poor ; and if I have taken any thing from any man by false accusation, I restore him fourfold.

And Jesus said unto him, This day is salvation come to this house, forasmuch as he also is a son of Abraham.

For the Son of man is come to seek and to save that which was lost.

And as they heard these things, He added and spake a parable, because He was nigh to Jerusalem, and because they thought that the kingdom of God should immediately appear.

He said therefore, A certain nobleman went into a far country to receive for himself a kingdom, and to return.

And he called his ten servants, and delivered them ten pounds, and said unto them, Occupy till I come.

But his citizens hated him, and sent a message after him, saying, We will not have this *man* to reign over us.

And it came to pass, that when he was returned, having received the kingdom, then he commanded these servants to be called unto him, to whom he had given the money, that he might know how much every man had gained by trading.

Then came the first, saying, Lord, thy pound hath gained ten pounds.

And he said unto him, Well, thou good servant: because thou hast been faithful in a very little, have thou authority over ten cities.

And the second came, saying, Lord, thy pound hath gained five pounds.

And he said likewise to him, Be thou also over five cities.

And another came, saying, Lord, behold, *here is* thy pound, which I have kept laid up in a napkin:

For I feared thee, because thou art an austere man: thou takest up that thou layedst not down, and reapest that thou didst not sow.

And he said unto him, Out of thine own mouth will I judge thee, *t h o u* wicked s e r v a n t . Thou knewest t h a t I was an austere man, taking up that I laid not down, and reaping t h a t I did not sow:

Wherefore t h e n gavest not thou my money into the bank, that at my coming I might have required mine own with usury?

And he said unto them that stood by, Take from him the pound, and give *it* to him that hath ten pounds.

(And they said unto him, Lord, he hath ten pounds.)

For I say unto you, That unto every one which hath, shall be given; and from him that hath not, even that he hath shall be taken away from him.

But those mine enemies, which would not that I should reign over t h e m , bring hither, and slay *them* before me.

And when He had thus spoken, He went before, ascending up to Jerusalem.

CHAPTER XXXII.

JESUS SUPS WITH MARY, MARTHA AND LAZARUS.

A ND the Jews' passover was nigh at hand: and many went out of the country up to Jerusalem before the passover to purify themselves.

Then sought they for Jesus, and spake among themselves as they stood in the temple, What think ye, that He will not come to the feast?

Now both the chief priests and the Pharisees had given a commandment, that if any man knew where He were, he should shew *it*, that they might take Him.

Then Jesus, six days before the passover, came to Bethany, where Lazarus was which had been dead, whom He raised from the dead.

Much people of the Jews also knew that He was there: and they came not for Jesus' sake only, but that they might see Lazarus also, whom He had raised from the dead.

But the chief priests consulted that they might put Lazarus also to death; because that by reason of him, many of the Jews went away and believed on Jesus.

And Jesus, being in Bethany, in the house of Simon the leper, they made Him a supper; and Martha served; but Lazarus was one of them that sat at the table with Him.

Then took Mary an alabaster box of very precious ointment of spikenard, very costly, and she brake the box, and poured *it* on His head as He sat at meat, and anointed the feet of Jesus, and wiped His feet with her hair: and the house was filled with the odour of the ointment.

But when His disciples saw *it*, there were some that had indignation within themselves, and murmured against her, saying, To what purpose *is* this waste?

Then saith one of His disciples, (Judas Iscariot, Simon's *son*, which should betray Him,) Why was not this ointment sold for three hundred pence, and given to the poor?

This he said, not that he cared for the poor; but because he was a thief, and had the bag, and bare what was put therein.

Then said Jesus, Let her alone; why trouble ye her? she hath wrought a good work on me: against the day of my burying hath she kept this.

For ye have the poor with you always, and whensoever ye will, ye may do them good: but me ye have not always.

She hath done what she could:

For in that she hath poured this ointment on my body, she is come aforehand to anoint my body for the burial.

Verily I say unto you, Wheresoever this gospel shall be preached throughout the whole world, *there* shall also this that she hath done, be told for a memorial of her.

And it came to pass on the next day, when they drew nigh unto Jerusalem, and were come unto Bethphage, unto the mount of Olives, much people that were come to the feast, when they heard that Jesus was coming to Jerusalem,

Took branches of palm trees, and went forth to meet Him, and cried, Hosanna! Blessed *is* the king of Israel that cometh in the name of the Lord!

Then sent Jesus forth two of His disciples, and saith unto them, Go your way into the village over against you; and as soon as ye be entered into it, straightway ye shall find an ass tied and a colt with her, whereon never man sat: loose *them*, bring *them* unto me.

And if any man say unto you, Why do ye this? say ye, The Lord hath need of them, and straightway he will send them.

And the disciples that were sent went their way, and found the colt even as He had said unto them, tied by the door without, in a place where two ways met; and they loose him.

And as they were loosing the colt, the owners thereof that stood there, said unto them, What do ye, loosing the colt?

And they said, The Lord hath need of him; even as Jesus had commanded: and they let them go.

And they brought the ass and the colt to Jesus, and cast their garments upon the colt, and they set Jesus thereon.

All this was done, that it might be fulfilled which was spoken by the prophets, saying,

"Tell ye the daughter of Sion, Fear not; behold, thy king cometh unto thee, meek, and sitting upon an ass, and a colt the foal of an ass."

These things understood not His disciples at the first: but when Jesus was glorified, then remembered they that these things were written of Him, and *that* they had done these things unto Him.

The people therefore that was with Him when He called Lazarus out of his grave, and raised him from the dead, bare record.

For this cause the people also met Him, for that they

"The Lord hath need of them."

heard that He had done this miracle.

CHRIST RIDETH INTO JERUSALEM

And as He went, a very great multitude spread their garments in the way; others cut down branches from the trees, and strewed *them* in the way.

And when He was come nigh, even now at the descent of the mount of Olives, the whole multitude of the disciples, and the multitudes that went before, and that followed, began to rejoice and praise God with a loud voice for all the mighty works that they had seen;

And cried, saying, Hosanna to the Son of David! Hosanna in the highest! Blessed *be* the king that cometh in the name of the Lord! peace in heaven, and glory in the highest!

Blessed *be* the kingdom of our father David, that cometh in the name of the Lord! Hosanna in the highest!

The Pharisees therefore said among themselves, Perceive ye how ye prevail nothing? behold, the world is gone after Him.

And some of the Pharisees from among the multitude said unto Him, Master, rebuke thy disciples.

And He answered and said unto them, I tell you that, if these should hold their peace, the stones would immediately cry out.

And when He was come near He beheld the city, and wept over it, saying, If thou hadst known, even thou, at least in this thy day, the things *which belong* unto thy peace! but now they are hid from thine eyes.

For the days shall come upon thee, that thine enemies shall cast a trench about thee, and compass thee round and keep thee in on every side, and shall lay thee even with the ground, and thy children within thee;

And they shall not leave in thee one stone upon another; because thou knewest not the time of thy visitation.

And when He was come into Jerusalem all the city was moved, saying, Who is this?

And the multitude said This is Jesus the prophet of Nazareth of Galilee.

And He went into the temple, and began to cast out them that sold therein, and them that bought; and overthrew the tables of the money-changers, and the seats of them that sold doves; and would not suffer that any man should carry *any* vessel through the temple; saying unto them,

Is it not written, "My house shall be called of all nations the house of prayer?" but ye have made it a den of thieves.

And the scribes and chief priests heard *it*, and sought how they might destroy Him: and could not find what they might do: for all the people were astonished at His doctrine, and were very attentive to hear Him.

And the blind and the lame came to Him in the temple; and He healed them.

And when the chief priests and scribes saw the wonderful things that He did, and the children crying in the temple, and saying, Hosanna to the Son of David! they were sore displeased,

And said unto Him,

Hearest thou what these say? And Jesus saith unto them, Yea; have ye never read, "Out of the mouth of babes and sucklings Thou hast perfected praise?"

And when He had looked round about upon all things, and now the eventide was come, He left them, and went out of the city unto Bethany with the twelve, and He lodged there.

CHAPTER XXXIII.

THE FRUITLESS FIG TREE.

AND on the morrow, in the morning, when they were come from Bethany, as He returned into the city, He hungered.

And when He saw a fig tree in the way, afar off, having leaves, He came, if haply he might find any thing thereon: and when He came to it, He found nothing but leaves; for the time of figs was not *yet*.

And Jesus said unto it, Let no fruit grow on the tree henceforward for ever. And His disciples heard *it*. And presently the fig tree withered away.

And they came to Jerusalem: and it came to pass as He taught the people in the temple and preached the gospel, the chief priests and the scribes came upon *Him* with the elders, and spake unto Him, saying, Tell us by what authority doest thou these things, and who gave thee this authority.

And Jesus answered and said unto them, I will also ask of you one question: the baptism of John, whence was it? from heaven or of men? Answer me, and I in likewise will tell you by what authority I do these things.

And they reasoned with themselves saying, If we shall say from heaven, He will say, Why then did ye not believe him? but if we shall say of men, all the people will stone us; for they be persuaded that John was a prophet indeed.

And they answered and said unto Jesus, We cannot tell whence *it was*. And Jesus said unto them, Neither do I tell you by what authority I do these things.

But what think ye? A *certain* man had two sons; and he came to the first, and said, Son, go work to-day in my vineyard.

He answered and said, I will not; but afterward he repented, and went.

And he came to the second, and said likewise. And he answered and said, I *go*, sir; and went not.

Whether of them twain did the will of *his* father? They say unto Him, The first. Jesus saith unto them, Verily I say unto you, that the publicans and the harlots go into the kingdom of God before you.

For John came unto you in the way of righteousness, and ye believed him not; but the publicans and the harlots believed him: and ye, when ye had seen *it*, repented not afterward, that ye might believe him.

Hear another parable: There was a certain householder, which planted a vineyard, and hedged it round about, and digged a winepress in it, and built a tower, and let it out to husbandmen, and went into a far country for a long time.

And when the time of the fruit drew near, he sent to the husbandmen a servant, that he might receive

And the multitude said, This is Jesus the prophet of Nazareth of Galilee.

from the husbandmen of the fruit of the vineyard.

And the husbandmen caught *him*, and beat him, and sent *him* away empty.

And again he sent unto them another servant; and at him they cast stones, and wounded *him* in the head, and entreated *him* shamefully, and sent *him* away empty.

And again he sent a third: and him they killed, and many others; beating some and killing some.

Then said the Lord of the vineyard, What shall I do? I will send my beloved son; it may be they will reverence *him* when they see him.

Having yet therefore one son, his well beloved, he sent him also last unto them, saying, They will reverence my son.

But when the husbandmen saw him they reasoned among themselves, saying, This is the heir; come, let us kill him, that the inheritance may be ours.

So they cast him out of the vineyard, and killed *him*.

When therefore the Lord of the vineyard cometh, what will he do unto those husbandmen? He will miserably destroy those wicked men, and will let out *his* vineyard unto other husbandmen, which shall render him the fruits in their seasons.

And when they heard *it*, they said, God forbid!

And He beheld them, and said, What is this then that is written? Did ye never read this Scripture: "The stone which the builders rejected, the same is become the head of the corner: this is the Lord's doing, and it is marvellous in our eyes?"

Therefore say I unto you,

The kingdom of God shall be taken from you, and given to a nation bringing forth the fruits thereof.

And whosoever shall fall on this stone shall be broken: but on whomsoever it shall fall, it will grind him to powder.

And when the chief priests and Pharisees had heard His parables, they perceived that He spake of them; and they sought the same hour to lay hold on Him, but feared the multitude, because they took Him for a prophet.

And they left Him, and went their way, and took counsel how they might entangle Him in *His* talk.

For though He had done so many miracles before them, yet they believed not on Him: that the saying of Esaias the prophet might be fulfilled, which he spake, "Lord, who hath believed our report? and to whom hath the arm of the Lord been revealed?"

Therefore they could not believe, because that Esaias said again, "He hath blinded their eyes, and hardened their heart; that they should not see with *their* eyes, nor understand with *their* heart, and be converted, and I should heal them."

These things said Esaias, when he saw His glory, and spake of Him.

Nevertheless among the chief rulers also many believed on Him; but because of the Pharisees they did not confess *Him*, lest they should be put out of the synagogue:

For they loved the praise of men more than the praise of God.

¶ And in the daytime He was teaching in the

The Mount of Olives.

temple; and at night He went out, and abode in the mount that is called *the mount* of Olives.

And all the people came early in the morning to Him in the temple, for to hear Him.

CHAPTER XXXIV.

AND as He returned into the city with His disciples, as they passed by, they saw the fig tree which He had cursed dried up from the roots; and when the disciples saw *it*, they marvelled;

And Peter calling to remembrance, saith unto Him, Master, behold, the fig tree which thou cursedst is whithered away!

And Jesus answering saith unto them, Have faith in God.

For verily I say unto you, If ye have faith, and doubt not, ye shall not only do this *which is done* to the fig tree, but also if ye shall say unto this mountain, Be thou removed, and be thou cast into the sea; it shall be done.

And all things, whatsoever ye shall ask in prayer, believing, ye shall receive.

Therefore I say unto you, What things, soever ye desire, when ye pray, believe that ye receive *them*, and ye shall have *them*.

And when ye stand praying, forgive, if ye have aught against any; that you Father also which is in heaven may forgive you your trespasses.

But if ye do not forgive, neither will your Father which is in heaven forgive your trespasses.

¶ And there were certain Greeks among them that came up to worship at the feast:

The same came therefore to Philip, which was of Bethsaida of Galilee, and desired him, saying, Sir, we would see Jesus.

Philip cometh and telleth Andrew : and again Andrew and Philip tell Jesus.

And Jesus answered them, saying, The hour is come, that the Son of man should be glorified.

Verily, verily, I say unto you, Except a corn of wheat fall into the ground and die, it abideth alone : but if it die, it bringeth forth much fruit.

He that loveth his life shall lose it ; and he that hateth his life in this world, shall keep it unto life eternal.

If any man serve me, let him follow me ; and where I am, there shall also my servant be ; if any man serve me, him will *my* Father honour.

Now is my soul troubled ; and what shall I say? Father, save me from this hour? but for this cause came I unto this hour. Father, glorify thy name.

A VOICE FROM HEAVEN

THEN came there a voice from heaven, *saying*, I have both glorified *it*, and will glorify *it* again.

The people therefore that stood by, and heard *it*, said that it thundered : others said, An angel spake to Him.

Jesus answered and said This voice came not because of me, but for your sakes.

Now is the judgment of this world : now shall the prince of this world be cast out.

And I, if I be lifted up from the earth, will draw all *men* unto me.

(This He said, signifying what death He should die.)

The people answered Him. We heard out of the law that Christ abideth forever: and how sayest thou, The Son of man must be lifted up! who is this Son of man?

Then Jesus said unto them, Yet a little while is the light, with you. Walk while ye have the light, lest darkness come upon you: for he that walketh in darkness knoweth not whither he goeth.

While ye have light, believe in the light, that ye may be the children of light.

He that believeth on me, believeth not on me, but on Him that sent me; and he that seeth me, seeth Him that sent me.

I am come a light into the world, that whosoever believeth on me should not abide in darkness.

And if any man hear my words, and believe not, I judge him not: for I came not to judge the world, but to save the world.

He that rejecteth me and receiveth not my words, hath one that judgeth him: the word that I have spoken, the same shall judge him in the last day.

For I have not spoken of myself; but the Father which sent me, He gave me a commandment, what I should say, and what I should speak.

And I know that His commandment is life everlasting: whatsoever I speak therefore, even as the Father said unto me, so I speak.

THE WIDOWS MITE

And Jesus sat over against the treasury; and He looked up, and beheld how the people cast money into the treasury: and many that were rich cast in much.

And there came a certain

poor widow, and she threw in two mites, which made a farthing.

And He called *unto Him* His disciples, and saith unto them, Verily I say unto you, That this poor widow hath cast more in, than all they which have cast into the treasury ;

For all *they* did cast in of their abundance unto the offerings of God : but she of her want did cast in all that she had, *even* all her living.

¶ And Jesus answered and spake unto them again by parables, and said,

The kingdom of heaven is like unto a certain king, which made a marriage for his son ;

And sent forth his servants to call them that were bidden to the wedding : and they would not come.

Again, he sent forth other servants, saying, Tell them which are bidden, Behold, I have prepared my dinner : my oxen and *my* fatlings *are* killed, and all things *are* ready : come unto the marriage.

But they made light of *it*, and went their ways, one to his farm, another to his merchandise :

And the remnant took his servants, and entreated *them* spitefully, and slew *them*.

But when the king heard *thereof*, he was wroth : and he sent forth his armies, and destroyed those murderers, and burned up their city.

Then saith he to his servants, The wedding is ready, but they which were bidden were not worthy.

Go ye therefore into the highways, and as many as ye shall find, bid to the marriage.

So those servants went out into the highways, and

The Widow's Mite

gathered together all as many as they found, both bad and good; and the wedding was furnished with guests.

And when the king came in to see the guests, he saw there a man which had not on a wedding garment:

And he saith unto him, Friend, how camest thou in hither not having a wedding garment? And he was speechless.

Then said the king to the servants, Bind him hand and foot, and take him away, and cast *him* into outer darkness; there shall be weeping and gnashing of teeth.

For many are called, but few *are* chosen.

TRIBUTE TO BE PAID TO CÆSAR

Then send the Pharisees unto Him spies, to catch Him in *His* words, (certain of their disciples with the Herodians,) which should feign themselves just men, that they might take hold of His words, that so they might deliver Him unto the power and authority of the governor.

And when they were come, they say unto Him, Master, we know that thou sayest and teachest rightly, that thou art true, and teachest the way of God in truth, neither carest thou for any *man*: for thou regardest not the person of men.

Tell us therefore, What thinkest thou? Is it lawful to give tribute unto Cæsar, or not?

But Jesus perceived their craftiness, and knowing their hypocrisy and wickedness, said unto them, Why tempt ye me, *ye* hypocrites? Shew me the tribute money; bring me a penny that I may see *it*. And they brought unto Him a penny.

And He saith unto them Whose image and superscription hath it? They say unto Him, Cæsar's.

Then saith He unto them, Render therefore unto Cæsar the things which are Cæsar's; and unto God the things that are God's.

When they had heard *these words*, they marvelled at Him, and held their peace;

And they could not take hold of His words before the people: and they marvelled at His answer, and left Him, and went their way.

DENIERS OF THE RESURRECTION SILENCED

The same day came to Him certain of the Sadducees, which deny that there is any resurrection; and they asked Him, saying,

Master, Moses wrote unto us, If any man's brother die, having a wife, and he die without children, that his brother should marry his wife, and raise up seed unto his brother.

Now there were with us seven brethren: and the first, when he had married a wife, died; and, having no issue, left his wife unto his brother:

And the second took her to wife, and he died childless.

And the third took her, and in like manner the seven also: and they left no children, and died.

Last of all the woman died also.

Therefore in the resurrection when they all shall rise, whose wife shall she be of the seven? for they all had her to wife.

"Cæsar the things which are Cæsar's; and unto things that are God's."

And Jesus answering said unto them, Ye do err, because ye know not the Scriptures, neither the power of God.

The children of this world marry, and are given in marriage: but they which shall be accounted worthy to obtain that world, and the resurrection from the dead, neither marry, nor are given in marriage:

Neither can they die any more: for they are equal unto the angels of God in heaven, and are the children of God, being the children of the resurrection.

But as touching the resurrection of the dead, have ye not read in the book of Moses, how in the bush God spake unto him, saying, "I *am* the God of Abraham, and the God of Isaac, and the God of Jacob?"

He is not the God of the dead, but the God of the living: for all live unto Him. Ye therefore do greatly err.

And when the multitude heard *this*, they were astonished at His doctrine.

CHAPTER XXXV.

A LAWYER NOT FAR FROM THE KINGDOM OF GOD.

THEN certain of the scribes answering said, Master, thou hast well said.

But when the Pharisees had heard that He had put the Sadducees to silence, they were gathered together.

Then one of the scribes, (a lawyer,) came, and having heard them reasoning together, and perceiving that He had answered them well, asked *Him a question*, tempting Him, and saying,

Master, which *is* the great commandment in the

law; the first commandment of all?

And Jesus answered him, The first of all the commandments *is*, "Hear. O Israel; The Lord our God is one Lord: and thou shalt love the Lord thy God with all thy heart, and with all thy soul, and with all thy mind, and with all thy strength:"

This is the first and great commandment.

And the second *is* like unto it, thou shalt love thy neighbour as thyself.

On these two commandments hang all the law and the prophets. There is none other commandment greater than these.

And the scribe said unto Him, Well, Master, Thou hast said the truth: for there is one God; and there is none other but He:

And to love Him with all the heart, and with all the understanding, and with all the soul, and with all the strength, and to love *his* neighbour as himself, is more than all whole burnt offerings and sacrifices.

And when Jesus saw that he answered discreetly, He said unto him, thou art not far from the kingdom of God. And no man after that durst ask Him *any question at all.*

WHILE the Pharisees were gathered together, Jesus asked them, saying, What think ye of Christ? whose son is He? They say unto Him, *The son* of David.

He said unto them, How then doth David in spirit call Him Lord?

For David himself said in the book of Psalms, by the Holy Ghost, "The Lord said to my Lord, 'Sit thou on my right hand, till I make thine enemies thy footstool.'"

David therefore himself calleth Him Lord; How is He then his son?

And no man was able to answer Him a word, neither durst any *man* from that day forth ask Him any more *questions*. And the common people heard Him gladly.

Then spake Jesus to the multitude, and to His disciples, saying, The scribes and the Pharisees sit in Moses' seat: all therefore whatsoever they bid you observe, *that* observe and do; but do not ye after their works: for they say, and do not.

For they bind heavy burdens and grievous to be borne, and lay *them* on men's shoulders; but they *themselves* will not move them with one of their fingers.

But all their works they do for to be seen of men.

They make broad their phylacteries, and enlarge the borders of their garments, and love the uppermost rooms at feasts, and the chief seats in the synagogues, and greetings in the markets, and to be called of men, Rabbi, Rabbi.

But be not ye called Rabbi: for one is your Master, *even* Christ; and all ye are brethren.

And call no *man* your father upon the earth: for one is your Father, which is in heaven.

Neither be ye called masters: for one is your Master, *even* Christ.

But he that is greatest among you, shall be your servant.

And whosoever shall exalt himself, shall be abased; and he that shall humble himself, shall be exalted.

But woe unto you, scribes and Pharisees, hypocrites! for ye shut up the kingdom of heaven against men: for ye neither go in *yourselves*, neither suffer ye them that are entering to go in.

Woe unto you, scribes and Pharisees, hypocrites! for ye devour widows' houses, and for a pretence make long prayer: therefore ye shall receive the greater damnation.

Woe unto you, scribes and Pharisees, hypocrites! for ye compass sea and land to make one proselyte; and when he is made, ye make him twofold more the child of hell than yourselves.

Woe unto you, *ye* blind guides! which say, Whosoever shall swear by the temple, it is nothing; but whosoever shall swear by the gold of the temple, he is a debtor.

Ye fools and blind: for whether is greater, the gold, or the temple that sanctifieth the gold?

And, Whosoever shall swear by the altar, it is nothing; but whosoever sweareth by the gift that is upon it, he is guilty.

Ye fools and blind: for whether *is* greater, the gift, or the altar that sanctifieth the gift?

Whoso therefore shall swear by the altar, sweareth by it, and by all things thereon.

And whoso shall swear by the temple, sweareth by it, and by Him that dwelleth therein.

And he that shall swear by heaven, sweareth by the throne of God, and by Him that sitteth thereon.

Woe unto you, scribes and Pharisees, hypocrites!

for ye pay tithe of mint and anise and cummin, and have omitted the weightier *matters* of the law, judgment, mercy, and faith: these ought ye to have done, and not to leave the other undone.

Ye blind guides, which strain at a gnat, and swallow a camel.

Woe unto you, scribes and Pharisees, hypocrites! for ye make clean the outside of the cup and of the platter, but within they are full of extortion and excess.

Thou blind Pharisee, cleanse first that *which is* within the cup and platter, that the outside of them may be clean also.

Woe unto you, scribes and Pharisees, hypocrites! for ye are like unto whited sepulchres, which indeed appear beautiful outward, but are within full of dead *men's* bones, and of all uncleanness.

Even so ye also outwardly appear righteous unto men, but within ye are full of hypocrisy and iniquity.

Woe unto you, scribes and Pharisees, hypocrites! because ye build the tombs of the prophets, and garnish the sepulchres of the righteous, and say, If we had been in the days of our fathers, we would not have been partakers with them in the blood of the prophets.

Wherefore ye be witnesses unto yourselves, that ye are the children of them which killed the prophets.

Fill ye up then the measure of your fathers.

Ye serpents, *ye* generation of vipers! how can ye escape the damnation of hell?

Wherefore behold, I send unto you prophets, and wise men, and scribes: and *some* of them ye shall kill and crucify; and *some* of them shall ye scourge in your synagogues, and persecute *them* from city to city:

That upon you may come all the righteous blood shed upon the earth, from the blood of righteous Abel unto the blood of Zacharias son of Barachias, whom ye slew between the temple and the altar.

Verily I say unto you, All these things shall come upon this generation.

O Jerusalem, Jerusalem, *thou* that killest the prophets, and stonest them which are sent unto thee, how often would I have gathered thy children together; even as a hen gathereth her chickens under *her* wings, and ye would not!

Behold, your house is left unto you desolate. For I say unto you, Ye shall not see me henceforth, till ye shall say, Blessed *is* he that cometh in the name of the Lord!

And Jesus went out, and departed from the temple: and did hide Himself from them.

CHAPTER XXXVI

CHRIST FORETELLETH THE DESTRUCTION OF THE TEMPLE.

AND as He went out of the temple, some spake of the temple, how it was adorned with goodly stones and gifts, and one of His disciples saith unto Him Master, see what manner of stones and what buildings *are here*!

And Jesus answering said unto him, Seest thou these great buildings? verily I say unto you, the days will come, in the which there shall not be left one

And Jesus went out and departed from the temple: and did hide Himself from them.

The common people heard Him gladly.

stone upon the other, that shall not be thrown down.

And as He sat upon the mount of Olives, over against the temple, Peter and James and John and Andrew came unto Him privately, saying,

Master, Tell us, when shall these things be? and what sign *will there be* when these things shall come to pass? and what *shall be* the sign of thy coming, and of the end of the world?

And Jesus answered and said unto them, Take heed that no man deceive you.

For many shall come in my name, saying, I am Christ; and shall deceive many.

The time draweth near: go ye not therefore after them.

But when ye shall hear of wars and rumors of wars, see that ye be not troubled: for *such things* must needs be; for all *these things* must first come to pass; but the end is not yet.

For nation shall rise against nation, and kingdom against kingdom: and there shall be famines, and pestilences, and great earthquakes, in divers places; and fearful sights and great signs shall there be from heaven.

All these *are* the beginning of sorrows.

But take heed to yourselves: for they shall lay their hands on you and persecute *you*, delivering *you* up to the synagogues, and into prisons:

They shall deliver you up to councils, to be afflicted, and shall kill you, and in the synagogues ye shall be beaten: and ye shall be brought before rulers and kings for my sake, for a testimony against them.

And ye shall be betrayed both by parents, and brethren, and kinsfolks, and friends; and *some* of you shall they cause to be put to death.

And ye shall be hated of all *men* for my name's sake.

But there shall not an hair of your head perish.

In your patience possess ye your souls.

But when they shall lead *you*, and deliver you up, take no thought beforehand what ye shall speak, neither do ye premeditate: but whatsoever shall be given you in that hour, that speak ye: for it is not ye that speak, but the Holy Ghost.

Settle *it* therefore in your hearts, not to meditate before what ye shall answer: for I will give you a mouth and wisdom, which all your adversaries shall not be able to gainsay nor resist.

And then shall many be offended, and shall betray one another, and shall hate one another.

The brother shall betray the brother to death, and the father the son; and children shall rise up against *their* parents, and shall cause them to be put to death.

And many false prophets shall rise, and shall deceive many.

And because iniquity shall abound, the love of many shall wax cold.

But he that shall endure unto the end, the same shall be saved.

And this gospel of the kingdom shall be preached in all the world for a witness unto all nations; and then shall the end come.

When ye therefore shall see the abomination of desolation, spoken of by Daniel the prophet, stand in the holy place, (whoso readeth, let him understand,) and when ye shall see Jerusalem compassed with armies, then know that the desolation thereof is nigh.

Then let them which are in Judea flee to the mountains; and let them which are in the midst of it depart out; and let not them that are in the countries enter thereinto.

And let him that is on the housetop not go down into the house, neither enter *therein*, to take any thing out of his house: neither let him which is in the field return back to take his clothes.

For these be the days of vengeance, that all things which are written may be fulfilled.

But woe unto them that are with child, and to them that give suck in those days! for there shall be great distress in the land, and wrath upon this people.

And they shall fall by the edge of the sword, and shall be led away captive into all nations; and Jerusalem shall be trodden down of the Gentiles, until the times of the Gentiles be fulfilled.

But pray ye that your flight be not in the winter, neither on the sabbath day: for then shall be great tribulation, such as was not since the beginning of the world which God created unto this time, no, nor ever shall be.

And except that the Lord had shortened those days, no flesh should be saved: but for the elect's sake, whom He hath chosen, He hath shortened the days.

And then if any man shall say to you, Lo, here *is* Christ; or, lo, *He is* there, believe *him* not: for false Christs and false prophets shall rise, and shall show signs and wonders, to seduce, if *it were* possible, even the elect.

But take ye heed: behold, I have foretold you all things.

Wherefore if they shall say unto you, Behold, He is in the desert; go not forth: behold, *He is* in the secret chambers; believe *it* not.

For as the lightning cometh out of the east, and shineth even unto the west; so shall also the coming of the Son of man be.

For wheresoever the carcass is, there will the eagles be gathered together.

Immediately after the tribulation of those days there shall be signs in the sun, and in the moon, and in the stars; and upon the earth distress of nations, with perplexity; the sea and the waves roaring;

Men's hearts failing them for fear, and for looking after those things which are coming on the earth: for the sun shall be darkened, and the moon shall not give her light, and the stars shall fall from heaven, and the powers of the heavens shall be shaken:

And then shall appear the sign of the Son of man in heaven: and then shall all the tribes of the earth mourn, and they shall see the Son of man coming in the clouds of heaven with power and great glory.

And He shall send His angels with a great sound of a trumpet, and they shall gather together His elect from the four winds, from the uttermost part of the earth to the uttermost part of heaven.

And when these things begin to come to pass, then look up, and lift up your heads; for your redemption draweth nigh.

Now learn a parable of the fig tree; When his branch is yet tender, and putteth forth leaves, ye see and know of your own selves that summer is now nigh at hand.

So likewise ye, when ye shall see all these things come to pass, know ye that the kingdom of God is nigh at hand, *even* at the doors.

Verily I say unto you, This generation shall not pass away, till all these things be fulfilled.

Heaven and earth shall pass away; but my words shall not pass away.

And take heed to yourselves, lest at any time your hearts be overcharged with surfeiting, and drunkenness, and cares of this life, and *so* that day come upon you unawares.

For as a snare shall it come on all them that dwell on the face of the whole earth.

Watch ye therefore, and pray always, that ye may be accounted worthy to escape all these things that shall come to pass, and to stand before the Son of man.

But of that day and *that* hour knoweth no man, no, not the angels which are in heaven, neither the Son, but my Father only.

Take ye heed, watch and pray; for ye know not when the time is.

For as the days of Noe *were*, so shall also the coming of the Son of man be.

For as in the days that were before the flood they were eating and drinking, marrying and giving in marriage, until the day that Noe entered into the ark, and knew not until the flood came, and took them all away; so shall also the coming of the Son of Man be.

Then shall two be in the field; the one shall be taken and the other left.

Two *women shall be* grinding at the mill; the one shall be taken, and the other left,

Watch therefore ; for ye know not what hour your Lord doth come.

But know this, that if the goodman of the house had known in what watch the thief would come, he would have watched, and would not have suffered his house to be broken up.

Therefore be ye also ready : for in such an hour as ye think not, the Son of man cometh.

For the Son of man is as a man taking a far journey, who left his house, and gave authority to his servants, and to every man his work, and commanded the porter to watch.

Who then is a faithful and wise servant, whom his lord hath made ruler over his household, to give them meat in due season ?

Blessed *is* that servant, whom his lord when he cometh shall find so doing.

Verily I say unto you, That he shall make him ruler over all his goods.

But and if that evil servant shall say in his heart, My lord delayeth his coming ; and shall begin to smite *his* fellow servants, and to eat and drink with the drunken ;

The lord of that servant shall come in a day when he looketh not for *him*, and in an hour that he is not aware of, and shall cut him asunder, and appoint *him* his portion with the hypocrites : there shall be weeping and gnashing of teeth.

Watch ye therefore : for ye know not when the

master of the house cometh, at even, or at midnight, or at the cockcrowing, or in the morning : lest coming suddenly, he find you sleeping !

And what I say unto you I say unto all, Watch !

CHAPTER XXXVII.

THE PARABLE OF THE TEN VIRGINS.

THEN shall the kingdom of heaven be likened unto ten virgins, which took their lamps, and went forth to meet the bridegroom.

And five of them were wise, and five *were* foolish.

They that *were* foolish took their lamps, and took no oil with them.

But the wise took oil in their vessels with their lamps.

While the bridegroom tarried, they all slumbered and slept.

And at midnight there was a cry made, Behold, the bridegroom cometh ; go ye out to meet him.

Then all those virgins arose, and trimmed their lamps.

And the foolish said unto the wise, Give us of your oil; for our lamps are gone out.

But the wise answered, saying, *Not so;* lest there be not enough for us and you; but go ye rather to them that sell, and buy for yourselves,

And while they went to buy, the bridegroom came ; and they that were ready went in with him to the marriage: and the door was shut,

Afterward came also the other virgins, saying, Lord, Lord, open to us.

But he answered and said, Verily I say unto you, I know you not.

Watch therefore; for ye know neither the day nor the hour wherein the Son of Man cometh.

PARABLE OF THE TALENTS

¶ For *the kingdom of heaven is* as a man travelling into a far country, *who* called his own servants, and delivered unto them his goods.

And unto one he gave five talents, to another two, and to another one; to every man according to his several ability; and straightway took his journey.

Then he that had received the five talents went and traded with the same, and made *them* other five talents.

And likewise he that *had received* two, he also gained other two.

But he that had received one went and digged in the earth, and hid his lord's money.

After a long time the lord of those servants cometh, and reckoneth with them.

And so he that had received five talents came and brought other five talents, saying, Lord, thou deliveredst unto me five talents: behold, I have gained beside them five talents more.

His lord said unto him, Well done, *thou* good and faithful servant: thou hast been faithful over a few things, I will make thee ruler over many things: enter thou into the joy of thy lord.

He also that had received two talents came and said, Lord, thou deliveredst unto me two talents: behold, I have gained two other talents beside them.

His Lord said unto him, Well done, good and faithful servant; thou hast been faithful over a few things, I

will make thee ruler over many things: enter thou into the joy of thy Lord.

Then he which had received the one talent came and said, Lord, I knew thee that thou art a hard man, reaping where thou hast not sown, and gathering where thou hast not strewed:

And I was afraid, and went and hid my talent in the earth: lo, *there* thou hast *that is* thine.

His lord answered and said unto him, *Thou* wicked and slothful servant, thou knewest that I reap where I sowed not, and gather where I have not strewed:

Thou oughtest therefore to have put my money to the exchangers, and *then* at my coming I should have received my own with usury.

Take therefore the talent from him, and give *it* unto him which hath ten talents.

For unto every one that hath shall be given, and he shall have abundance: but from him that hath not shall be taken away even that which he hath.

And cast ye the unprofitable servant into outer darkness: there shall be weeping and gnashing of teeth.

THE LAST JUDGMENT.

WHEN the Son of man shall come in His glory, and all the holy angels with him, then shall He sit upon the throne of His glory:

And before Him shall be gathered all nations: and He shall separate them one from another, as a shepherd divideth *his* sheep from the goats:

And He shall set the sheep on His right hand, but the goats on the left.

Then shall the King say unto them on his right hand, Come, ye blessed of my Father, inherit the kingdom prepared for you from the foundation of the world:

For I was a hungered, and ye gave me meat: I was thirsty, and ye gave me drink: I was a stranger, and ye took me in:

Naked, and ye clothed me: I was sick, and ye visited me: I was in prison, and ye came unto me.

Then shall the righteous answer Him, saying, Lord, when saw we thee a hungered, and fed *thee*? or thirsty, and gave *thee* drink?

When saw we thee a stranger, and took *thee* in? or naked, and clothed *thee*?

Or when saw we thee sick, or in prison, and came unto thee?

And the King shall answer and say unto them, **Verily** I say unto you, Inasmuch as ye have done *it* unto one of the least of these my brethren, ye have done *it* unto me.

Then shall He say also unto them on the left hand, Depart from me, ye cursed, into everlasting fire, prepared for the devil and his angels:

For I was a hungered, and ye gave me no meat: I was thirsty, and ye gave me no drink:

I was a stranger, and ye took me not in: naked, and ye clothed me not: sick, and in prison, and ye visited me not.

Then shall they also answer Him, saying, Lord, when saw we thee a hungered, or athirst, or a stranger, or naked, or sick, or in prison, and did not minister unto thee?

Then shall he answer them, saying, Verily I say unto you, Inasmuch as ye did *it* not to one of the least

"What will ye give me, and I will deliver Him unto you?"

of these, ye did *it* not to me.

And these shall go away into everlasting punishment: but the righteous into life eternal.

CHAPTER XXXVIII.

THE RULERS CONSPIRE AGAINST CHRIST.

AND it came to pass, when Jesus had finished all these sayings, He said unto His disciples,

Ye know that after two days is *the feast of* the passover, and the Son of man is betrayed to be crucified.

Then assembled together the chief priests, and the scribes, and the elders of the people, unto the palace of the high priest, who was called Caiaphas, and consulted that they might take Jesus by subtilty, and kill Him.

But they said, Not on the feast *day*, lest there be an uproar among the people; for they feared the people.

Then entered Satan into Judas surnamed Iscariot, being of the number of the twelve.

And he went his way, and communed with the chief priests and captains, how he might betray Him unto them;

And *said unto* them, What will ye give me, and I will deliver Him unto you?

And when they heard *it*, they were glad, and promised to give him money. And they covenanted with him for thirty pieces of silver.

And from that time he sought opportunity how he might conveniently betray Him unto them in the absence of the multitude.

Now the first *day* of the *feast of* unleavened bread,

when they killed the passover, the disciples came to Jesus, saying unto Him, where wilt thou that we prepare for thee to eat the passover?

And He sendeth forth two of His disciples, Peter and John, and saith unto them, Go ye into the city: and behold, when ye are entered into the city, there shall a man meet you, bearing a pitcher of water; follow him into the house where he entereth in.

And wheresoever he shall go in, say ye to the goodman of the house, the master saith, my time is at hand; I will keep the passover at thy house. Where is the guest chamber, where I shall eat, the passover with my disciples?

And he will shew you a large upper room furnished *and* prepared: there make ready for us.

And His disciples went forth, and came into the city, and found as He had said unto them: and they made ready the passover.

CHRIST EATETH THE PASSOVER WITH HIS DISCIPLES.

Now before the feast of the passover, when Jesus knew that His hour was come that He should depart out of this world unto the Father, having loved His own which were in the world, He loved them unto the end.

And in the evening He cometh with the twelve, and when the hour was come, He sat down, and the twelve apostles with Him.

And He said unto them, With desire I have desired to eat this passover with you before I suffer: for I say unto you, I will not any more eat thereof,

until it be fulfilled in the kingdom of God.

And He took the cup, and gave thanks, and said, Take this, and divide *it* among yourselves: for I say unto you, I will not drink of the fruit of the vine, until the kingdom of God shall come.

TEACHETH THEM HUMILITY AND CHARITY.

And there was a strife among them, which of them should be accounted the greatest.

And He said unto them, The kings of the Gentiles exercise lordship over them; and they that exercise authority upon them are called benefactors.

But ye *shall* not *be* so: but he that is greatest among you, let him be as the younger; and he that is chief, as he that doth serve.

For whether *is* greater, he that sitteth at meat, or he that serveth? *is* not he that sitteth at meat? but I am among you as he that serveth.

Ye are they which have continued with me in my temptations.

And I appoint unto you a kingdom, as my father hath appointed unto me;

That ye may eat and drink at my table in my kingdom, and sit on thrones judging the twelve tribes of Israel.

And supper being ended, (the devil having now put into the heart of Judas Iscariot, Simon's *son*, to betray Him;) Jesus, knowing that the Father had given all things into His hands, and that He was come from God, and went to God:

He riseth from supper, and laid aside His garment; and took a towel, and girded Himself.

After that, He poureth water into a basin, and began to wash the disciples' feet, and to wipe *them* with the towel wherewith He was girded.

Then cometh He to Simon Peter: and Peter saith unto Him, Lord, dost thou wash my feet?

Jesus answered and said unto him, what I do thou knowest not now; but thou shalt know hereafter.

Peter saith unto Him, Thou shalt never wash my feet! Jesus answered him, If I wash thee not, thou hast no part with me.

Simon Peter saith unto Him, Lord, not my feet only, but also *my* hands and *my* head.

Jesus saith to him, He that is washed needeth not save to wash *his* feet, but is clean every whit: and ye are clean, but not all.

(For He knew who should betray Him; therefore said He, Ye are not all clean.)

So after He had washed their feet, and had taken His garments, and was set down again, He said unto them, Know ye what I have done to you?

Ye call me master and Lord: and ye say well; for *so* I am.

If I then, *your* Lord and Master, have washed your feet; ye also ought to wash one another's feet.

For I have given you an example, that ye should do as I have done to you.

Verily, verily, I say unto you, The servant is not greater than his lord; neither he that is sent greater than he that sent him.

If ye know these things happy are ye if ye do them.

I speak not of you all: I know whom I have chosen:

"For I have given you an example, that ye should do as I have done to you."

but that the Scripture may be fulfilled. "He that eateth bread with me hath lifted up his heel against me."

Now I tell you before it come, that, when it is come to pass, ye may believe that I am *He*.

Verily, verily, I say unto you, He that receiveth whomsoever I send, receiveth me; and he that receiveth me, receiveth Him that sent me.

THE BETRAYER.

WHEN Jesus had thus said, He was troubled in spirit, and testified, and said, Verily, verily, I say unto you, that one of you which eateth with me shall betray me! behold, the hand of him that betrayeth me *is* with me on the table.

And they began to inquire among themselves, which of them it was that should do this thing, and were exceedingly sorrowful, and began every one of them to say unto Him, one by one, Lord, is it I?

And He answered and said, One of the twelve that dippeth *his* hand with me in the dish, the same shall betray me.

The Son of man indeed goeth, as it was determined; and as it is written of Him, but woe unto that man by whom the Son of man is betrayed! it had been good for that man if he had never been born.

Then the disciples looked one on another, doubting of whom He spake.

Now there was leaning on Jesus' bosom one of His disciples, whom Jesus loved.

Simon Peter therefore beckoned to him, that he should ask who it should be of whom He spake.

He then lying on Jesus'

breast, s a i t h unto Him, Lord, who is it?

Jesus answered, He it is, to whom I shall give a sop, when I have dipped *it*. And when He had dipped the sop, He gave *it* to Judas Iscariot, *the son* of Simon.

Then Judas, which betrayed Him, answered and said, Master, is it I? He said unto him, Thou hast said.

And after the sop, Satan entered i n t o him. Then said Jesus unto him, That thou doest, do quickly.

Now no man at the table knew for what intent He spake this unto him.

For some *of them* thought, because Judas had the bag, that Jesus had said unto him, Buy *those things* that we have need of against the feast ; or, that he should give s o m e t h i n g to the poor.

He then having received the sop, went immediately out ; and it was night.

Therefore, when he was gone out, Jesus said, Now is the Son of man glorified, and God is glorified in Him.

If God be glorified in Him, God shall also glorify Him in Himself, and shall straightway glorify Him.

Little children, yet a little while I am with you. Ye shall seek me; and as I said unto the Jews, Whither I go, ye cannot come; so now I say to you.

A new commandment I give unto you, That ye love one another; as I have loved you, that ye also love one another.

By this shall all *men* know that ye are my disciples, if ye have love one to another.

Simon Peter said unto Him, Lord, whither goest thou? Jesus answered him, Whither I go, thou canst not follow me now; but thou shalt follow me afterwards.

Peter said unto Him Lord, why cannot I follow Thee, now? I will lay down my life for thy sake.

Jesus answered him, Wilt thou lay down thy life for my sake? Verily, verily, I say unto thee, The cock shall not crow, till thou hast, denied me thrice.

"THIS DO IN REMEMBRANCE OF ME"

And as they were eating, Jesus took b r e a d, and blessed *it*, and brake *it*, and gave *it* to the disciples, and said, Take, eat ; this is my body, which is given for you : this do in remembrance of me.

Likewise also He took the cup after supper, and when He had given thanks, He gave *it* to them : saying, drink ye all of it. And they all drank of it.

And He said unto them, this is my blood of the new testament, which is shed for you and for many, for the remission of sins ; this do ye, as often as ye drink *it*, in remembrance of me.

But I say unto you, I will not drink, henceforth of this fruit of the vine, until that day when I drink it new with you in my Father's kingdom.

CHAPTER XXXIX.

CHRIST COMFORTETH HIS DISCIPLES WITH THE HOPE OF HEAVEN.

LET not your heart be troubled : ye believe in God, believe also in me.

In my Father's house are many mansions : if *it were* not *so*, I would have told you. I go to prepare a place for you.

And if I go and prepare a place for you, I will come

again and receive you unto myself; that where I am, *there* ye may be also.

And whither I go ye know, and the way ye know.

Thomas saith unto Him, Lord, we know not whither thou goest; and how can we know the way?

Jesus saith unto him, I am the way, the truth, and the life: no man cometh unto the Father but by me.

If ye had known me, ye should have known my Father also: and from henceforth ye know Him and have seen Him.

Philip saith unto Him, Lord, shew us the Father and it sufficeth us.

Jesus saith unto him, Have I been so long with you, and yet hast thou not known me, Philip? he that hath seen me hath seen the Father; and how sayeth thou *then*, Shew us the Father?

Believest thou not that I am in the Father, and the Father in me? the words that I speak unto you I speak not of myself: but the Father that dwelleth in me, He doeth the works.

Believe me that I *am* in the Father, and the Father in me: or else believe me for the very works' sake.

Verily, verily, I say unto you, He that believeth on me, the works that I do shall he do also; and greater *works* than these shall he do; because I go unto my Father.

And whatsoever ye shall ask in my name, that will I do, that the Father may be glorified in the Son.

If ye shall ask anything in my name, I will do *it*.

¶ If ye love me, keep my commandments.

And I will pray the Father, and He shall give

The Way, the Truth, the Life.

you another Comforter, that He may abide with you forever;

Even the Spirit of truth ; whom the world cannot receive, because it seeth Him not, neither knoweth Him : but ye know Him ; for He dwelleth w i t h you, and shall be in you.

I will not leave you comfortless : I will come to you.

Yet a little while, and the world s e e t h me no more ; but ye see me : because I live, ye shall live also.

At that day ye shall know that I *am* in my Father, and ye in me, and I in you.
He that hath my commandments, and keepeth them, he it is that loveth me : and he that loveth me shall be loved of my Father, and I will love him, and will manifest myself to him.

Judas saith unto him, not Iscariot, Lord, how is it that thou wilt manifest thyself unto us, and not unto the world ?

Jesus answered and said unto him, If a man love me, he will keep my words : and my Father will love him, and we will come unto him, and make our abode with him.

He that loveth me not keepeth not my sayings : and the word which ye hear is not mine, but the Father's which sent me.

These t h i n g s have I spoken unto you, being *yet* present with you.

But the Comforter, *which is* the Holy Ghost, whom the Father will send in my name, He shall teach you all things, and bring all things to your rememberance, whatsoever I have said unto you.

Peace I leave with you, my peace I give unto you : not as the world giveth, give

I unto you. Let not your heart be troubled, neither let it be afraid.

Ye have heard how I said unto you, I go away, and come *again* unto you. If ye loved me, ye would rejoice, because I said, I go unto the Father: for my Father is greater than I.

And now I have told you before it come to pass, that when it is come to pass, ye might believe.

Hereafter I will not talk much with you: for the prince of this world cometh and hath nothing in me.

But that the world may know that I love the Father; and as the Father gave me commandment, even so I do. Arise, let us go hence.

THE PARABLE OF THE VINE.

I AM the true vine, and my Father is the husbandman.

Every branch in me that beareth not fruit He taketh away: and every *branch* that beareth fruit He purgeth it, that it may bring forth more fruit.

Now ye are clean through the word which I have spoken unto you.

Abide with me, and I in you. As the branch cannot bear fruit of itself, except it abide in the vine; no more can ye, except ye abide in me.

I am the vine, ye *are* the branches. He that abideth in me and I in him, the same bringeth forth much fruit; for without me ye can do nothing.

If a man abide not in me, he is cast forth as a branch, and is withered; and men gather them and cast *them* into the fire, and they are burned.

If ye abide in me, and my words in you, ye shall ask what ye will, and it shall be done unto you.

Herein is my Father glorified, that ye bear much fruit; so shall ye be my disciples.

As the Father hath loved me, so have I loved you: continue ye in my love.

If ye keep my commandments, ye shall abide in my love; even as I have kept my Father's commandments, and abide in His love.

These things have I spoken unto you, that my joy might remain in you, and *that* your joy might be full.

This is my commandment, That ye love one another, as I have loved you.

Greater love hath no man than this, that a man lay down his life for his friends.

Ye are my friends, if ye do whatsoever I command you.

Henceforth I call ye not servants; for the servant knoweth not what his lord doeth: but I have called you friends; for all things that I have heard of my Father I have made known unto you.

Ye have not chosen me, but I have chosen you and ordained you, that ye should go and bring forth fruit, and *that* your fruit should remain: that whatsoever ye shall ask of the Father in my name, He may give it you.

These things I command you, that ye love one another.

If the world hate you, ye know that it hated me before *it hated* you.

If ye were of the world, the world would love his own; but because ye are not of the world, but I have chosen you out of the world, therefore the world hateth you.

Remember the word that I said unto you, The servant is not greater than his lord. If they have persecuted me, they will also persecute you; if they have kept my saying, they will keep yours also.

But all these things will they do unto you for my name's sake, because they know not Him that sent me.

If I had not come and spoken unto them, they had not had sin: but now they have no cloak for their sin.

He that hateth me hateth my Father also.

If I had not done among them the works which none other man did, they had not had sin: but now have they both seen and hated both me and my Father.

But *this cometh to pass*, that the word might be fulfilled that is written in their law, They hated me without a cause.

But when the Comforter is come, whom I will send unto you from the Father, *even* the Spirit of truth, which proceedeth from the Father, He shall testify of me:

And ye also shall bear witness, because ye have been with me from the beginning.

CHRIST PROMISES THE HOLY GHOST AS A COMFORTER AND GUIDE.

These things have I spoken unto you, that ye should not be offended.

They shall put you out of the synagogues: yea, the time cometh, that whosoever killeth you will think he doeth God service.

And these things will

they do unto you, because they have not known the Father, nor me.

But these things have I told you, that when the time shall come, ye may remember that I told you of them. And these things I said not unto you at the beginning, because I was with you.

But now I go my way to Him that sent me; and none of you asketh me, Whither goest thou?

But because I have said these things unto you, sorrow hath filled your heart.

Nevertheless I tell you the truth; It is expedient for you that I go away: for if I go not away the Comforter will not come unto you; but if I depart, I will send Him unto you.

And when He is come He will reprove the world of sin, and of righteousness, and of judgment:

Of sin, because they believe not on me;

Of righteousness, because I go to my Father, and ye see me no more;

Of judgment, because the prince of this world is judged.

I have yet many things to say unto you, but ye cannot bear them now.

Howbeit when He, the Spirit of truth, is come, He will guide you into all truth: for He shall not speak of Himself; but whatsoever He shall hear, *that* shall He speak: and He wilt shew you things to come.

He shall glorify me: for He shall receive of mine, and shall shew *it* unto you.

All things that the Father hath are mine: therefore said I, that He shall take of mine, and shall shew *it* unto you.

A little while and ye shall

not see me: and again a little while, and ye shall see me, because I go to the Father.

Then said *some* of His disciples among themselves, What is this that He saith unto us, A little while and ye shall not see me: and again a little while, and ye shall see me: and, Because I go to the Father.

They said therefore, What is this that He saith, A little while? we cannot tell what He saith.

Now Jesus knew that they were desirous to ask Him, and said unto them, Do you inquire among yourselves of that I said, A little while and ye shall not see me: and again a little while, and ye shall see me?

Verily, Verily, I say unto you, That ye shall weep and lament, but the world shall rejoice; and ye shall be sorrowful, but your sorrow shall be turned into joy.

A woman when she is in travail hath sorrow, but as soon as she is delivered of the child, she remembereth no more the anguish for joy that a man is born into the world.

And ye now therefore have sorrow: but I will see you again, and your heart shall rejoice, and your joy no man taketh from you.

And in that day ye shall ask me nothing. Verily, verily, I say unto you, Whatsoever ye shall ask the Father in my name He will give *it* you.

Hitherto have ye asked nothing in my name: ask and ye shall receive, that your joy may be full.

These things have I spoken unto you in proverbs: but the time cometh, when I shall no more speak unto you in proverbs, but I

shall shew you plainly of the Father.

At that day ye shall ask in my name: and I say unto you, that I will pray the Father for you:

For the Father himself loveth you, because ye have loved me, and have believed that I came out from God.

I came forth from the Father, and come into the world: again, I leave the world, and go to the Father.

His disciples said unto him, Lo, now speakest thou plainly, and speakest no proverb.

Now are we sure that thou knowest all things, and needest not that any man should ask thee: by this we believe that thou camest forth from God.

Jesus answered them, Do ye now believe?

Behold, the hour cometh, yea, is now come, that ye shall be scattered, every man to his own, and shall leave me alone: and yet I am not alone, because the Father is with me.

These things I have spoken unto you, that in me ye might have peace. In the world ye shall have tribulation: but be of good cheer; I have overcome the world.

CHAPTER XL.

CHRIST PRAYETH FOR ALL WHO SHALL BELIEVE ON HIM IN THE AGES TO COME.

THESE words spake Jesus and lifted up His eyes to heaven, and said, Father, the hour is come; glorify thy Son, that thy Son may glorify thee.

As thou hast given Him power over all flesh, that He should give eternal life to as many as thou hast given Him.

And this is life eternal, that they might know thee the only true God, and Jesus Christ, whom thou hast sent.

I have glorified thee on the earth : I have finished the work which thou gavest me to do.

And now, O Father, glorify thou me with thine own self with the glory which I had with thee before the world was.

I have manifested thy name unto the men which thou gavest me out of the world : thine they were, and thou gavest them to me ; and they have kept thy word.

Now they have known that all things whatsoever thou hast given me are of thee.

For I have given unto them the words which thou gavest me ; and they have received *them*, and have known surely that I came out from thee, and they have believed that thou didst send me.

I pray for them : I pray not for the world, but for them which thou hast given me ; for they are thine.

And all mine are thine, and thine are mine, and I am glorified in them.

And now I am no more in thee world, but these are in the world, and I come to thee. Holy Father, keep through thine own name those whom thou hast given me, that they may be one, as we *are*.

While I was with them in the world, I kept them in thy name : those that thou gavest me I have kept, and none of them is lost, but the son of perdition ; that the Scripture might be fulfilled.

And now come I to thee; and these things I speak in the world, that they might have my joy fulfilled in themselves.

I have given them thy word; and the world hath hated them, because they are not of the world, even as I am not of the world.

I pray not that thou shouldest take them out of the world, but that thou shouldest keep them from the evil.

They are not of the world, even as I am not of the world.

Sanctify them through thy truth; thy word is truth.

As thou hast sent me into the world, even so have I also sent them into the world.

And for their sakes I sanctify myself, that they also might be sanctified through the truth.

Neither pray I for these alone, but for them also which shall believe on me through their word;

That they all may be one; as thou, Father, *art* in me, and I in thee, that they also may be one in us: that the world may believe that thou hast sent me.

And the glory which thou gavest me I have given them; that they may be one, even as we are one:

I in them, and thou in me, that they may be made perfect in one; and that the world may know that thou hast sent me, and hast loved them, as thou hast loved me.

Father, I will that they also, whom thou hast given me, be with me where I am; that they may behold my glory, which thou hast given me: for thou lovedst me before the foundation of the world.

O righteous Father, the world hath not known thee: but I have known thee, and these have known that thou hast sent me.

And I have declared unto them thy name, and will declare *it;* that the love wherewith thou hast loved me may be in them and I in them.

CHAPTER XLI.

HIS BETRAYAL.

WHEN Jesus had spoken these words, and when they had sung a hymn, He went forth, as he was wont, with His disciples over the brook Cedron.

Then said Jesus unto them, All ye shall be offended because of me this night: for it is written, "I will smite the shepherd, and the sheep of the flock shall be scattered abroad." But after I am risen again I will go before you into Galilee.

Peter answered and said unto Him, Though all *men* shall be offended because of thee, *yet* will I never be offended.

And the Lord said, Simon, Simon, behold Satan hath desired *to have* you, that he may sift *you* as wheat: but I prayed for thee that thy faith fail not: and when thou are converted, strengthen thy brethren.

And he said unto Him, Lord, I am ready to go with thee, both into prison and to death.

And He said, I tell thee, Peter, That this day, *even* in this night, before the cock crow twice, thou shalt thrice deny that thou knowest me.

But he spoke the more vehemently, If I should die

with thee, I will not deny thee in any wise. Likewise also said all the disciples.

And He said unto them, When I sent you without purse, and scrip, and shoes, lacked ye anything? And they said, Nothing.

Then said He unto them, But now, he that hath a purse, let him take *it*, and likewise *his* scrip: and he that hath no sword, let him sell his garment, and buy one.

For I say unto you, that this that is written must yet be accomplished in me, "And He was reckoned among the transgressors:" for the things concerning me have an end.

And they said, Lord, behold, here *are* two swords. And He said unto them, It is enough.

The cometh Jesus with them unto the mount of Olives, where was a garden, called Gethsemane: into the which He entered, and His disciples.

(And Judas also, which betrayed Him, knew the place: for Jesus ofttimes resorted thither with His disciples.)

And He said unto them, Pray that ye enter not into temptation. Sit ye here, while I go and pray yonder.

And He took with Him, Peter and the two sons of Zebedee, James and John, and began to be sore amazed, and to be very heavy;

Then saith He unto them, My soul is exceeding sorrowful, even unto death: tarry ye here and watch with me.

And He went forward a little further, and was withdrawn from them about a stone's cast, and kneeled down, and fell on His face on the ground, and prayed that, if it were possible, the hour might pass from Him.

And He said, Abba, Father, all things *are* possible unto thee; O my Father, if it be possible, if thou be willing, remove this cup from me: nevertheless, not my will, but thine, be done.

And there appeared an angel unto Him from heaven, strengthening Him.

And being in an agony, He prayed more earnestly: and His sweat was as it were great drops of blood falling down to the ground.

And He rose up from prayer, and cometh unto the disciples, and findeth them sleeping from sorrow; and saith unto them, Why sleep ye? rise and pray, lest ye enter into temptation.

And He saith unto Peter, Simon, sleepest thou? couldest not thou watch with me one hour?

Watch and pray, that ye enter not into temptation: the spirit indeed *is* willing, but the flesh *is* weak.

He went away again the second time, and prayed, and spake the same words, saying, O my Father, if this cup may not pass away from me, except I drink it, thy will be done.

And He came and found them asleep again: (for their eyes were heavy,) neither wist they what to answer Him.

And He left them, and went away again, and prayed the third time, saying the same words.

Then cometh He to His disciples the third time, and saith unto them, Sleep on now, and take *your* rest: it is enough; behold, the hour is at hand, and the Son of man is betrayed into the hands of sinners.

Rise, let us be going: be-

"O my Father, if this cup may not pass away from me, except I drink thy will be done."

And Judas also which betrayed Him knew the place.

"Rise, let us be going: behold, he is at hand that doth betray me."

"Judas, betrayest thou the Son of man with a kiss?"

hold, he that betrayeth me is at hand.

And immediately, while He yet spake, lo, Judas, one of the twelve, having received a band *of men* and officers from the chief priests and Pharisees, cometh thither with lanterns and torches and weapons;

And with him a great multitude with swords and staves, from the chief priests and the scribes and the elders of the people.

Now he that betrayed Him had given them a token, saying, Whomsoever I shall kiss, that same is He; take Him, hold Him fast, and lead *Him* away safely.

And as soon as he was come, he went before them. and drew near unto Jesus, and saith, Hail, master, and kissed Him.

And Jesus said unto him, Friend, wherefore art thou come? Judas, betrayeth thou the Son of man with a kiss?

Then Jesus, knowing all things that should come upon Him, went forth and said unto them, Whom seek ye?

They answered Him, Jesus of Nazareth. Jesus saith unto them, I am *He*.

As soon then as He had said unto them, I am *He*, they went backward and fell to the ground.

Then asked He them again, Whom seek ye? And they said, Jesus of Nazareth.

Jesus answered, I have told you that I am *He:* if therefore ye seek me, let these go their way : (that the saying might be fulfilled which He spake, Of them which thou gavest me have I lost none.)

Then came they and laid

hands on Jesus, and took Him.

When they which were about Him saw what would follow, they said unto Him, Lord, shall we smite with the sword?

Then Simon Peter, having a sword, drew it, and smote a servant of the high priest, and cut off his right ear. The servant's name was Malchus.

And Jesus answered and said, Suffer ye thus far. And He touched his ear, and healed him.

Then said Jesus unto Peter, Put up thy sword into the sheath: for all they that take the sword shall perish with the sword. The cup which my Father hath given me, shall I not drink it?

Thinkest thou that I cannot now pray to my Father, and He shall presently give me more than twelve legions of angels?

But how then shall the Scriptures be fulfilled, that thus it must be?

In that same hour Jesus said unto the chief priests, and captains of the temple, and the elders, which were come to Him, Be ye come out, as against a thief, with swords and staves to take me?

When I was daily with you in the temple, ye stretched forth no hands against me: but this is your hour, and the power of darkness.

Then all the disciples forsook Him, and fled.

And there followed Him a certain young man, having a linen cloth cast about *his* naked *body;* and the young men laid hold on him: and he left the linen cloth, and fled from them naked.

Then the band and the captain and officers of the Jews, led Jesus away to Annas first; for he was father-in-law to Caiaphas, which was the high priest that same year.

Annas then asked Jesus of His disciples, and of His doctrine.

Jesus answered him, I spake openly to the world; I ever taught in the synagogue, and in the temple, whither the Jews always resort; and in secret have I said nothing.

Why askest thou me? ask them which heard me, what I have said unto them: behold, they know what I said.

And when He had thus spoken, one of the officers which stood by, struck Jesus with the palm of his hand, saying, Answerest thou the high priest so?

Jesus answered him, If I have spoken evil, bear witness of the evil; but if well, why smitest thou me?

Then took they Him, and led *Him* away bound, unto Caiaphas the high priest, and brought Him into the high priest's house, where were assembled all the chief priests and the elders and the scribes.

(Now Caiaphas was he, which gave counsel to the Jews, that it was expedient that one man should die for the people.)

And Peter followed afar off, and *so did* another disciple: that disciple was known unto the high priest, and went in with Jesus into the palace of the high priest.

But Peter stood at the door without. Then went out that other disciple, which was known unto the high priest, and spake unto her that kept the door, and brought in Peter.

And the servants and officers stood there, who had made a fire of coals in the midst of the hall, for it was cold; and they warmed themselves: and when they were set down together, Peter sat down among them and warmed himself.

Now the chief priests and elders, and all the council, sought false witness against Jesus that they might put Him to death; but found none; yea, though many false witnesses came, yet their witness agreed not together.

At the last came two false witnesses, and bare false witness against Him, saying,

We heard Him say, I will destroy this temple that is made with hands, and within three days I will build another made without hands.

But neither so did their witness agree together.

And the high priest arose and stood up in the midst, and asked Jesus, saying, Answerest thou nothing? what *is it which* these witness against thee?

But Jesus held His peace and answered nothing. Again the high priest answered and said unto Him, I adjure thee by the living God, that thou tell us whether thou be the Christ, the Son of God.

And Jesus said, I am: and ye shall see the Son of man sitting on the right hand of power, and coming in the clouds of heaven.

Then the high priest rent his clothes, saying, He hath spoken blasphemy! what further need have we of witnesses? behold now ye have heard His blasphemy: what think ye? And they all condemned Him to be guilty of death.

Then did they spit in His face, and buffeted Him: and the servants did strike Him with the palms of their hands;

And the men that held Jesus mocked Him, and smote *Him;* and when they had blindfolded Him, they struck Him on the face, saying, Prophesy unto us, thou Christ, Who is he that smote thee?

And many other things blasphemously spake they against Him.

¶ Now Peter sat with the servants, to see the end, and warmed himself at the fire.

And the damsel that kept the door, (one of the maids of the high priest,) beheld him as he sat by the fire, and earnestly looked upon him, and said, Art not thou also *one* of this man's disciples? Thou also wast with Jesus of Galilee.

But he denied before *them* all, saying, Woman, I know Him not; neither understand I what thou sayest. And he went out into the porch; and the cock crew.

And after a little while another maid saw him, and began to say to them that stood by, This is *one* of them; this *fellow* was also with Jesus of Nazareth.

They said therefore unto him, Art not thou also *one* of His disciples?

And again he denied with an oath, I do not know the man.

And about the space of one hour after, another confidently affirmed, saying, Of a truth this *fellow* also was with Him; for he is a Galilean.

And they that stood by said again to Peter, Surely

thou art *one* of them: for thou art a Galilean, and thy speech betrayeth thee.

One of the servants of the high priest, being *his* kinsman whose ear Peter cut off, saith, Did not I see thee in the garden with Him?

Then began he to curse and to swear, *saying*, Man, I know not what thou sayest; I know not this man of whom ye speak. And immediately, while he yet spake, the cock crew.

And the Lord turned, and looked upon Peter. And Peter remembered the word of the Lord, how He had said unto him, Before the cock crow twice, thou shalt deny me thrice.

And Peter went out, and wept bitterly.

CHAPTER XLII.

CHRIST IS DELIVERED TO PILATE.

AND straightway in the morning, as soon as it was day, the chief priests held a consultation with the elders of the people, and the scribes, and the whole council, and took counsel against Jesus to put Him to death. And they led Him into their council, saying,

Art thou the Christ? tell us. And He said unto them, If I tell you, ye will not believe: and if I also ask *you*, ye will not answer me, nor let *me* go.

Hereafter shall the Son of man sit on the right hand of the power of God.

Then said they all. Art thou the Son of God? And He said unto them, Ye say that I am.

And they said, What need we any further wit-

And Peter went out and wept bitterly.

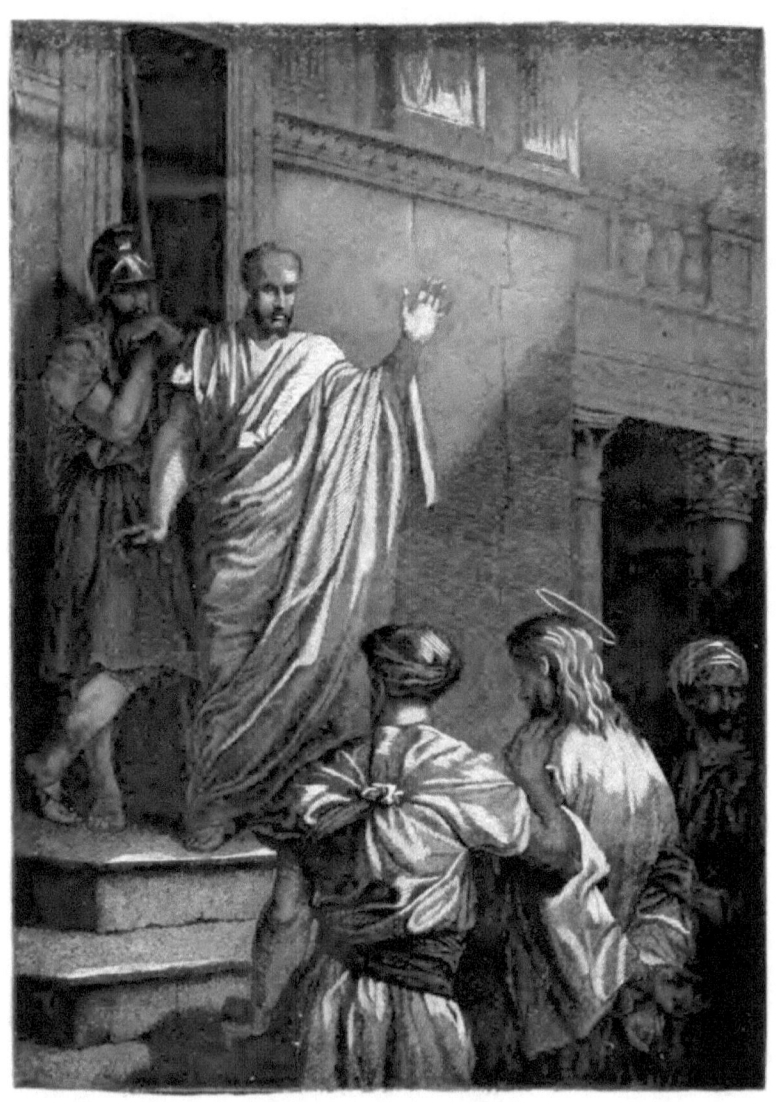

Jesus brought before Pilate.

nesses? for we ourselves have heard of His own mouth.

And the whole multitude of them arose, and when they had bound Jesus, they led *Him* unto the hall of judgment, and delivered Him to Pontius Pilate the governor.

Then Judas, which had betrayed Him, when he saw that He was condemned, repented himself, and brought again the thirty pieces of silver to the chief priests and elders, saying, I have sinned in that I have betrayed the innocent blood.

And they said, What *is that* to us: see thou to *that*.

JUDAS HANGETH HIMSELF.

And he cast down the pieces of silver in the temple, and departed, and went and hanged himself.

And the chief priests took the silver pieces, and said, It is not lawful for to put them into the treasury, because it is the price of blood.

And they took counsel, and bought with them the potter's field, to bury strangers in. Wherefore that field was called, The field of blood, unto this day.

Then was fulfilled that which was spoken by Jeremy the prophet, saying, "And they took the thirty pieces of silver, the price of Him that was valued, whom they of the children of Israel did value; and gave them for the potter's field, as the Lord appointed me."

And Jesus stood before the governor; and it was early; and the Jews themselves went not into the judgment hall, lest they should be defiled; but that they might eat the passover.

Pilate then went out unto them, and said, What accusation bring ye against this man?

They answered and said unto him, If He were not a malefactor, we would not have delivered Him up unto thee.

Then said Pilate unto them, Take ye Him, and judge Him according to your law. The Jews therefore said unto him, It is not lawful for us to put any man to death:

(That the saying of Jesus might be fulfilled, which He spake, signifying what death He should die.)

And they began to accuse Him, saying, We found this *fellow* perverting the nation and forbidding to give tribute to Cæsar, saying that He Himself is Christ a king.

And when He was accused, He answered nothing. Then said Pilate unto Him, Answerest thou nothing? Hearest thou not how many things they witness against thee?

And He answered him to never a word: insomuch that the governor marvelled greatly.

Then Pilate entered into the judgment hall again, and called Jesus and said unto Him, Art thou the king of the Jews:

Jesus answered him, Sayeth thou this thing of thyself, or did others tell it thee of me?

Pilate answered, Am I a Jew? Thine own nation and the chief priests have delivered thee unto me: what hast thou done?

Jesus answered him, My kingdom is not of this world: if my kingdom were of this world, then would my servants fight, that I should not be delivered to

"What *is that* to us: see thou *to that*."

the Jews: but now is my kingdom not from hence.

Pilate therefore said unto Him, Art thou a king then? Jesus answered, Thou sayest that I am a king. To this end was I born, and for this cause came I into the world, that I should bear witness unto the truth. Every one that is of the truth heareth my voice.

Pilate saith unto Him, What is truth? And when he had said this, he went out again, and saith unto the chief priests and to the people, I find in Him no fault *at all*.

And they were the more fierce, saying, He stirreth up the people, teaching throughout all Jewry, beginning from Galilee to this place.

When Pilate heard of Galilee, he asked whether the man were a Galilean.

And as soon as he knew that He belonged unto Herod's jurisdiction, he sent Him to Herod, who himself also was at Jerusalem at that time.

And when Herod saw Jesus, he was exceeding glad: for he was desirous to see Him of a long *season*, because he had heard many things of Him; and he hoped to have seen some miracle done by Him.

Then he questioned with Him in many words; but He answered him nothing.

And the chief priests and scribes stood and vehemently accused Him.

And Herod with his men of war set Him at nought, and mocked *Him*, and arrayed Him in a gorgeous robe, and sent Him again to Pilate.

And the same day Pilate and Herod were made friends together; for before, they were at enmity between themselves.

When Pilate was set down on the judgment seat, his wife sent unto him, saying, Have thou nothing to do with that just man: for I have suffered many things this day in a dream because of Him.

And Pilate, when he had called together the chief priests and the rulers and the people, said unto them,

Ye have brought this man unto me, as one that perverteth the people; and, behold, I, having examined *Him* before you, have found no fault in this man touching those things whereof ye accuse Him:

No, nor yet Herod; for I sent you to Him; and, lo, nothing worthy of death is done untoHim.

I will therefore chastise Him and release *Him*.

Now at *that* feast the governor was wont to release unto the people a prisoner, whomsoever they desired.

And they had then a notable prisoner called Barabbas, (who for a certain sedition made in the city, and for murder committed in the insurrection, was cast into prison; who *lay* bound with them that had made insurrection with him.)

And the multitude crying aloud began to desire *him to do* as he had ever done unto them; (for of necessity he must release one unto them at the feast).

Therefore when they were gathered together, Pilate said unto them, Ye have a custom that I should release unto you one at the passover. Whom will ye that I release unto you?

(For he knew that the chief priests had delivered Him for envy.)

But the chief priests and elders persuaded the multitude that they should ask that he should release Barabbas unto them and destroy Jesus. And they cried out all at once, saying Away with this *man*, and release unto us Barabbas!

Pilate therefore, willing to release Jesus, spake again to them.

Then cried they all again, saying, Not this man, but Barabbas! Now Barabbas was a robber.

And Pilate answered and said again unto them, What will ye then that I shall do with Jesus which is called Christ? *They* all cried out, Crucify Him! crucify Him!

Then said Pilate unto them the third time, Why, what evil hath He done? And they cried out the more exceedingly, Crucify Him.

And he said unto them, I have found no cause of death in Him: I will therefore chastise Him, and let Him go.

Pilate therefore took Jesus, and scourged *Him*.

¶ Then the soldiers of the governor took Jesus into the common hall, called Pretorium; and gathered unto Him the whole band.

And they stripped Him, and put on Him a purple robe.

And when they had platted a crown of thorns, they put *it* upon His head, and a reed in His right hand: and they bowed the knee before Him, and mocked Him, saying, Hail, King of the Jews!

And they spit upon Him, and took the reed, and smote Him on the head.

And when they had blindfolded Him, they struck Him on the face, and asked

Him, saying, Prophesy, who is it that smote thee?

Then came Jesus forth, wearing the crown of thorns, and the purple robe. And *Pilate* saith unto them, Behold the man!

When the chief priests therefore and officers saw Him, they cried out, saying, Crucify *Him!* crucify *Him!* Pilate saith unto them, Take ye Him, and crucify *Him:* for I find no fault in Him.

The Jews answered him, We have a law, and by our law He ought to die, because He made Himself the Son of God.

When Pilate therefore heard that saying, he was the more afraid; and went again into the judgment hall, and saith unto Jesus, Whence art thou? But Jesus gave him no answer.

Then said Pilate unto Him, Speakest thou not unto me? knowest thou not that I have power to crucify thee, and have power to release thee?

Jesus answered, Thou couldest have no power *at all* against me, except it were given thee from above; therefore he that delivered me unto thee hath the greater sin.

And from thenceforth Pilate sought to release Him: but the Jews cried out, saying, If thou let this man go, thou art not Cæsar's friend: whosoever maketh himself a king, speaketh against Cæsar.

When Pilate therefore heard that saying, he brought Jesus forth and sat down in the judgment seat in a place that is called the Pavement, but in the Hebrew Gabbatha.

And it was the preparation of the passover, and about the sixth hour: and

Pilate therefore took Jesus and scourged Him.

"Hail, King of the Jews."

he saith unto the Jews, Behold your king!

But they cried out, Away with *Him!* away with *Him!* crucify Him! Pilate saith unto them, Shall I crucify your king?

The chief priests answered, We have no king but Cæsar! And they were instant with loud voices, requiring that He might be crucified.

When Pilate saw that he could prevail nothing, but that rather a tumult was made, he took water and washed his hands before the multitude, saying, I am innocent of the blood of this just person : see ye *to it.*

Then answered all the people and said, His blood *be* on us and on our children!

And the voices of them and of the chief priests prevailed : and Pilate, willng to content the people, gave sentence that it should be as they required.

And he released unto them him that for sedition and murder was cast into prison, whom they had desired; but he delivered Jesus to their will.

And after that they had mocked Him, they took the robe off from Him and put His own raiment on Him, and led Him away to crucify *Him.*

CHRIST CRUCIFIED BETWEEN TWO THIEVES.

And He, bearing His cross, went forth.

And there followed Him a great company of people, and of women, which also bewailed and lamented Him.

And Jesus turning unto them, said, Daughters of Jerusalem, weep not for me, but weep for yourselves and for your children.

For behold the days are coming, in the which they shall say, Blessed *are* the barren, and the wombs that never bare, and the paps that never gave suck.

Then shall they begin to say to the mountains, Fall on us; and to the hills, Cover us.

For if they do these things in a green tree, what shall be done in the dry?

And there were also two others, malefactors, led with Him to be put to death.

And when they were come unto a place called Calvary, which is called in the Hebrew, Golgotha, that is to say, a place of a skull, they gave Him wine mingled with myrrh; and when He had tasted *thereof*, He would not drink.

And there they crucified Him, and the malefactors with Him, one on the right hand and the other on the left, and Jesus in the midst.

And the Scripture was fulfilled, which saith, "And He was numbered with the trangressors."

Then said Jesus, Father, forgive them; for they know not what they do!

And the soldiers, when they had crucified Jesus, took His garments, and made four parts, to every soldier a part; and also *His* coat: now the coat was without seam, woven from the top throughout.

They said therefore among themselves, Let us not rend it, but cast lots for it, whose it shall be: (that the Scripture might be fulfilled, which was spoken by the prophet,

"They parted my garments among them, and for my vesture they did cast lots.") These things therefore the soldiers did.

"Daughters of Jerusalem, weep not for me, but weep for yourselves, and for your children."

"They parted my garments among them, and upon my vesture did they cast lots."

And it was the third hour when they crucified Him; and sitting down, t h e y watched Him there.

And Pilate wrote a title, and put on the cross over His head His accusation. And the writing was, THIS IS JESUS OF NAZA- RETH, THE KING OF THE JEWS.

This title then read many of the Jews; (for the place where Jesus was crucified was nigh to the city;) and it was written in Hebrew, *and* Greek, *and* Latin.

Then s a i d t h e chief priests of the Jews to Pilate, Write not, The King of the Jews; but that He said I am King of the Jews.

Pilate answered, What I have written I have written.

And the people stood be- holding. And the rulers also with t h e m derided *H i m*, saying, He saved others, let Him save Him- self, if He be Christ, the chosen of God.

And the soldiers also mocked Him, coming to Him, and offering Him vinegar, and saying, If thou be the King of the Jews, save thyself!

And they that passed by reviled Him, and railed on Him, wagging their heads, and saying, Ah, thou that destroyest the temple, and buildest *it* in three days, save thyself! If thou be the Son of God, come down from the cross!

Likewise also the chief priests mocking *Him*, with the scribes and elders, said, He saved others, Himself He cannot save!

Let Christ the King of Israel descend now from the cross, that we may see, and we will believe Him.

He trusted in God: let Him deliver Him now, if

He will have Him : for He said, I am the Son of God.

And one of the thieves also which were crucified with Him, cast the same in His teeth, and railed on Him, saying, If thou be Christ, save thyself and us.

But the other answering rebuked him, saying, Dost not thou fear God, seeing thou art in the same condemnation?

And we indeed justly; for we receive the due reward of our deeds : but this man hath done nothing amiss.

And he said unto Jesus, Lord, remember me when thou comest into thy kingdom.

And Jesus said unto him, Verily I say unto thee, to-day shalt thou be with me in paradise.

¶ Now there stood by the cross of Jesus His mother and His mother's sister, Mary the *wife* of Cleophas, and Mary Magdalene.

When Jesus therefore saw His mother, and the disciple standing by, whom He loved, He saith unto His mother, Woman, behold thy son!

Then saith He to the disciple, Behold thy mother! And from that hour that disciple took her unto his own *home*.

Now from the sixth hour there was darkness over all the land unto the ninth hour.

And about the ninth hour Jesus cried with a loud voice, saying, Eli, Eli, lama sabachthani? that is to say, My God, my God, why hast thou forsaken me?

Some of them that stood there, when they heard *that*, said, This *man* calleth for Elias.

Now there stood by the cross of Jesus his mother, and his mother's sister, Mary the *wife* of Cleophas, and Mary Magdalene.

And straightway one of them ran, and took a sponge, and filled *it* with vinegar, and put *it* on a reed, and gave Him to drink.

The rest said, Let be, let us see whether Elias will come to save Him.

When Jesus therefore had received the vinegar, He said, It is finished : and when He had cried again with a loud voice, He said, Father, into thy hands I commend my spirit : and having said thus, He bowed His head, and yielded up the ghost.

And, behold, the vail of the temple was rent in twain in the midst, from the top to the bottom, and the earth did quake, and the rocks rent, and the graves were opened.

Now when the centurion, and they that were with him, watching Jesus, saw the earthquake and those things that were done, they feared greatly, saying, Truly this was the Son of God.

And the centurion glorified God, saying, Certainly this was a righteous man.

And all the people that came together to that sight, beholding the things which were done, smote their breasts and returned.

And all His acquaintance and the women that followed Him from Galilee, ministering unto Him, and came up with Him unto Jerusalem, stood afar off, beholding these things ;

Among them was Mary Magdalene, and Mary the mother of James the less and of Joses, and Salome, the mother of Zebedee's children, and many other women, who also, when He was in Galilee followed Him and ministered unto Him.

The Jews therefore, because it was the preparation, that the bodies should not remain upon the cross on the sabbath day (for that Sabbath day was an high day,) besought Pilate that their legs might be broken, and *that* they might be taken away.

Then came the soldiers and brake the legs of the first, and of the other which was crucified with Him.

But when they came to Jesus and saw that He was dead already, they brake not His legs: but one of the soldiers with a spear pierced His side, and forthwith came there out blood and water.

And he that saw *it* bare record, and his record is true; for he knoweth that he saith true, that ye might believe.

For these things were done, that the Scripture should be fulfilled, "A bone of Him shall not be broken."

And again another Scripture saith, "They shall look on Him whom they pierced."

JOSEPH OF ARIMATHEA.

AND behold, *there was* a rich man of Arimathea a city of the Jews, named Joseph, an honourable counsellor, a good and just man;

(The same had not consented to the counsel and deed of them,) who also himself waited for the kingdom of God.

And now when the even was come, because it was the preparation, that is, the day before the sabbath, this *man*, being a disciple of Jesus, but secretly for fear of the Jews, came, and went in boldly unto Pilate, and craved the body of Jesus.

And when Joseph had taken the body, he wrapped it in a clean linen cloth, and laid it in his own new tomb, which he had hewn out in the rock.

And Pilate marvelled if He were already dead: and calling *unto him* the centurion, he asked him whether He had been any while dead.

And when he knew *it* of the centurion, he commanded the body to be delivered to Joseph.

Joseph therefore bought fine linen, and took down the body of Jesus, and wrapped it in a clean linen cloth;

And there came also Nicodemus, (which at the first came to Jesus by night,) and brought a mixture of myrrh and aloes, about a hundred pound *weight*.

Then took they the body of Jesus, and wound it in linen clothes with the spices, as the manner of the Jews is to bury.

And when Joseph had taken the body, he laid it in his own new tomb, which he had hewn out in the rock: and he rolled a great stone to the door of the sepulchre and departed.

THE FAITHFUL WOMEN.

AND the women also, Mary Magdalene and the other Mary, *the mother* of Joses, which came with Him from Galilee, followed after, and sitting over against the sepulchre, beheld the sepulchre and how his body was laid.

And that day was the preparation, and the sabbath drew on.

And they returned and prepared spices and ointments; and rested the sabbath day according to the commandment.

¶ Now the next day that followed the day of the preparation, the chief priests and the Pharisees came together unto Pilate, saying, Sir, We remember that that deceiver said while He was yet alive, After three days I will rise again.

Command therefore that the sepulchre be made sure until the third day, lest His disciples come by night and steal Him away, and say unto the people, He is risen from the dead : so the last error shall be worse than the first.

Pilate said unto them, Ye have a watch : go your way, make *it* as sure as ye can.

So they went and made the sepulchre sure, sealing the stone and setting a watch.

And when the sabbath was past Mary Magdalene, and Mary the mother of James, and Salome, brought sweet spices, that they might come and anoint Him.

And as it began to dawn toward the first day of the week, behold there was a great earthquake : for the angel of the Lord descended from heaven, and came and rolled back the stone from door and sat upon it.

His countenance was like lightning, and his raiment white as snow : and for fear of him the keepers did shake and became as dead *men*.

And many bodies of the saints which slept, arose, and came out of the graves, and went into the holy city and appeared unto many.

¶ And very early in the morning, when it was yet dark, came Mary Magdalene and the other Mary to the sepulchre, bringing the spices which they had prepared, and certain other women with them.

And they said among themselves, Who shall roll

"Destroy this temple, and in three days I will raise it up."

And they said among themselves, Who shall roll us away the stone from the door of the sepulchre?

away the stone from the door of the sepulchre?

And when they looked, they saw that the stone was rolled away: for it was very great.

Then runneth Mary Magdalene and cometh to Simon Peter, and to the other disciple whom Jesus loved, and saith unto them, They have taken away the Lord out of the sepulchre, and we know not where they have laid Him!

But the other women entered into the sepulchre, and saw a young man sitting on the right side, clothed in a long white garment; and they were affrighted.

And the angel answered and said unto the women, Fear not ye: for I know that ye seek Jesus of Nazareth, which was crucified: He is not here: for He is risen as He said! Behold the place where they laid Him.

And go quickly and tell His disciples and Peter, that He is risen from the dead; and behold, He goeth before you into Galilee as He said unto you; there shall ye see Him: lo, I have told you!

And they went out quickly and fled from the sepulchre: for they trembled and were amazed.

And behold, two men stood by them in shining garments. And as they were afraid, and bowed down *their* faces to the earth, they said unto them, Why seek ye the living among the dead? He is not here, but is risen!

Remember how He spake unto you when He was yet in Galilee, saying, The Son of man must be delivered into the hands of sinful men, and be crufied, and the third day rise again.

And they remembered His words, and departed quickly from the sepulchre with fear and great joy: neither said they anything to any *man*, for they were afraid, but did run to bring His disciples word.

Now when they were going, behold, some of the watch came into the city and shewed unto the chief priests all the things that were done.

And when they were assembled with the elders, and had taken counsel, they gave large money unto the soldiers, saying, Say ye, His disciples came by night, and stole Him *away* while we slept.

And if this come to the governor's ears, we will persuade him, and secure you.

So they took the money, and did as they were taught: and this saying is commonly reported among the Jews until this day.

Now when Mary Magdalene came to Simon Peter, and to the other disciple, whom Jesus loved, and saith unto them, They have taken away the Lord out of the sepulchre, and we know not where they have laid Him, then arose Peter, and went forth, and that other disciple, and came to the sepulchre.

So they ran both together: and the other disciple did outrun Peter, and came first to the sepulchre.

And he stooping down, *and looking in*, saw the linen clothes lying; yet went he not in.

Then cometh Simon Peter following him, and went into the sepulchre, and seeth the linen clothes laid by themselves;

Jesus saith unto her, Mary. She turned herself, and saith unto him, Rabboni; which is to say, Master.

And the napkin that was about His head, not lying with the linen clothes, but wrapped together in a place by itself.

Then went in also that other disciple, which came first to the sepulchre, and he saw, and believed.

For as yet they knew not the Scripture, that He must rise again from the dead.

Then the disciples went away again unto their own home, wondering at that which was come to pass.

But Mary stood without at the sepulchre weeping: and as she wept, she stooped down *and looked* into the sepulchre, and seeth two angels in white sitting, the one at the head, and the other at the feet, where the body of Jesus had lain.

And they say unto her, Woman, why weepest thou? She saith unto them, Because they have taken away my Lord, and I know not where they have laid Him.

And when she had thus said, she turn herself back and saw Jesus standing, and knew not that it was Jesus.

Jesus saith unto her, Woman, why weepest thou? whom seekest thou? She, supposing Him to be the gardener, saith unto Him, Sir, if thou hast borne Him hence, tell me where thou hast laid Him, and I will take Him away.

Jesus saith unto her, Mary. She turned herself, and saith unto Him, Rabboni! which is to say, Master!

Jesus saith unto her, Touch me not; for I am not yet ascended to my Father: but go to my brethren and say unto them, I ascend unto my Father and your Father, and *to* my God and your God.

Mary Magdalene came and told the disciples that she had seen the Lord, and *that* He had spoken these things unto her.

CHAPTER XLIII.

NOW when *Jesus* was risen early on the first *day* of the week, He appeared first to Mary Magdalene, out of whom He had cast seven devils.

And she went and told them that had been with Him, as they mourned and wept.

And they, when they had heard that He was alive, and had been seen of her, believed not.

And as Joanna, and Mary *the mother* of James, and the other *women that were* with them, went to tell His disciples, behold, Jesus met them, saying, All hail!

And they came and held Him by the feet and worshipped Him.

Then said Jesus unto them, Be not afraid: go tell my brethren that they go into Galilee, and there they shall see me.

And they went and told all these things unto the eleven and to all the rest; and their words seemed to them as idle tales, and they believed them not.

After that He appeared in another form unto two of them, that same day, as they walked into the country to a village called Emmaus, which was from Jerusalem *about* threescore furlongs.

And they talked together of all these things which had happened.

And it came to pass that while they communed *together* and reasoned, Jesus

Himself drew near and went with them. But their eyes were holden that they should not know Him.

And He said unto them, What manner of communications *are* these that ye have one to another, as ye walk and are sad?

And the one of them, whose name was Cleopas, answering said unto Him, Art thou only a stranger in Jerusalem, and hast not known the things which are come to pass there in these days?

And He said unto them, What things? And they said unto Him, Concerning Jesus of Nazareth, which was a prophet mighty in deed and word before God and all the people:

And how the chief priests and our rulers delivered Him to be condemned to death, and have crucified Him.

But we trusted that it had been He which should have redeemed Israel: and beside all this, to-day is the third day since these things were done.

Yea, and certain women also of our company made us astonished, which were early at the sepulchre;

And when they found not His body, they came, saying, that they had also seen a vision of angels, which said that He was alive.

And certain of them which were with us, went to the sepulchre, and found *it* even so as the women had said: but Him they saw not.

Then He said unto them, O fools, and slow of heart to believe all that the prophets have spoken!

Ought not Christ to have suffered these things, and to enter into His glory?

And beginning at Moses

and all the prophets, He expounded unto them in all the Scriptures, the things concerning Himself.

And they drew nigh unto the village whither they went, and He made as though He would have gone further : but they constrained Him, saying, Abide with us : for it is toward evening and the day is far spent.

And He went in to tarry with them.

And it came to pass as He sat at meat with them, He took bread and blessed *it*, and brake and gave to them.

And their eyes were opened and they knew Him ; and He vanished out of their sight.

And they said one to another, Did not our heart burn within us while He talked with us by the way, and while He opened to us the Scriptures ?

And they rose the same hour and returned to Jerusalem the same day at evening (being the first *day* of the week,) and found the eleven gathered together at meat, and them that were with them, saying, The Lord has risen indeed, and hath appeared to Simon.

And they told what things *were done* in the way, and how He was known of them in breaking of bread.

And as they spake these things, and when the doors were shut where the disciples were assembled for fear of the Jews, Jesus Himself stood in the midst of them, and saith unto them, Peace *be* unto you.

But they were terrified and affrighted, and supposed that they had seen a spirit.

And He said unto them, Why are ye troubled?

And their eyes were opened, and they knew Him; and He vanished out of their sight.

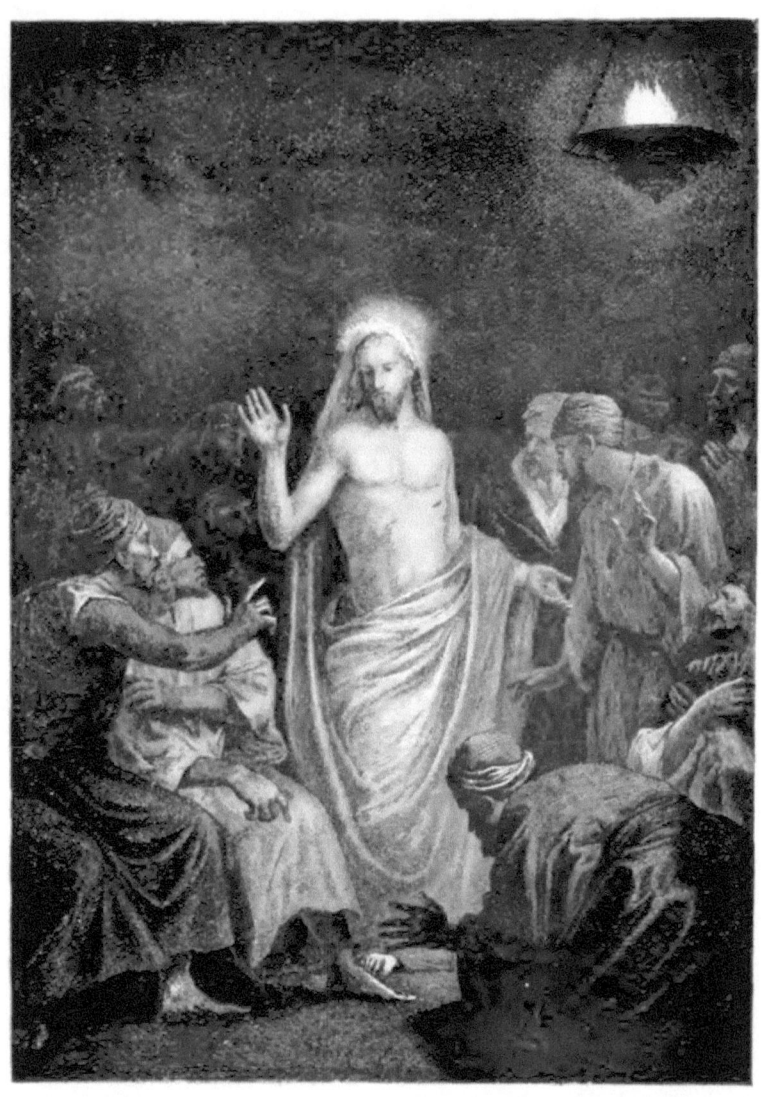

"Behold my hands and my feet that it is I myself; handle me and see."

and why do thoughts arise in your hearts?

Behold my hands and my feet, that it is I myself: handle me and see; for a spirit hath not flesh and bones, as ye see me have.

And when He had thus spoken, He shewed them *His* hands and feet, and His side. Then were the disciples glad, when they saw the Lord.

And while they yet believed not for joy, and wondered, He said unto them, Have ye here any meat?

And they gave Him a piece of a broiled fish, and of an honeycomb: and He took *it*, and did eat before them.

And He upbraided them with their unbelief and hardness of heart, because they believed not them which had seen Him after He was risen.

And He said unto them, These *are* the words which I spake unto you, while I was yet with you, that all things must be fulfilled, which were written in the law of Moses, and *in* the prophets, and *in* the psalms, concerning me.

Then opened He their understanding, that they might understand the Scriptures.

And said unto them, Thus it is written, and thus it behooved Christ to suffer, and to rise from the dead the third day:

And that repentance and remission of sins should be preached in His name among all nations, beginning at Jerusalem.

And ye are witnesses of these things.

And He said unto them, Go ye into all the world, and preach the gospel to every creature.

He that believeth and is

baptized shall be saved; but he that believeth not, shall be damned.

And these signs shall follow them that believe; In my name shall they cast out devils; they shall speak with new tongues; they shall take up serpents; and if they drink any deadly thing, it shall not hurt them; they shall lay hands on the sick, and they shall recover.

Then said Jesus to them again, Peace *be* unto you: as *my* Father hath sent me, even so send I you.

And when He had said this, He breathed on *them*, and saith unto them, Receive ye the Holy Ghost. Whosoever sins ye remit they are remitted unto them; *and* whosoever *sins* ye retain they are retained.

But Thomas, one of the twelve, called Didymus, was not with them when Jesus came.

The other disciples therefore said unto him, We have seen the Lord! But he said unto them, Except I shall see in His hands the print of the nails, and put my finger into the print of the nails, and thrust my hand into His side, I will not believe.

And after eight days, again His disciples were within, and Thomas with them: *then* came Jesus, the doors, being shut, and stood in the midst and said, Peace *be* unto you.

Then saith He to Thomas, Reach hither thy finger, and behold my hands; and reach hither thy hand, and thrust *it* into my side; and be not faithless but believing.

And Thomas answered and said unto Him, My Lord and my God.

"Blessed are they that have not seen, and yet have believed."

Jesus saith unto him, Thomas, because thou hast seen me, thou hast believed: blessed *are* they that have not seen, and *yet* have believed.

CHAPTER XLIV.

AFTER these things Jesus shewed Himself again to the disciples at the sea of Tiberias; and on this wise shewed he *himself.*

There were together Simon Peter, and Thomas called Didymus, and Nathanael of Cana in Galilee, and the *sons* of Zebedee, and two other of His disciples.

Simon Peter saith unto them, I go a fishing. They say unto him. We also go with thee. They went forth, and entered into a ship immediately; and that night they caught nothing.

But when the morning was now come, Jesus stood on the shore; but the disciples knew not that it was Jesus.

Then Jesus saith unto them, Children, have ye any meat? They answered him, No.

And He said unto them, Cast the net on the right side of the ship, and ye shall find. They cast therefore, and now they were not able to draw it for the multitude of fishes.

Therefore that disciple whom Jesus loved saith unto Peter, It is the Lord. Now when Simon Peter heard that it was the Lord, he girt *his* fisher's coat *unto him*, (for he was naked,) and did cast himself into the sea.

And the other disciples came in a little ship, (for they were not far from land, but as it were two hundred cubits,) dragging the net with fishes.

As soon then as they were come to land, they saw a fire of coals there, and fish laid thereon, and bread.

Jesus saith unto them, Bring of the fish which ye have now caught.

Simon Peter went up, and drew the net to land full of great fishes, a hundred and fifty and three: and for all there were so many, yet was not the net broken.

Jesus saith unto them, Come *and* dine. And none of the disciples durst ask Him, Who art thou? knowing that it was the Lord.

Jesus then cometh, and taketh bread, and giveth them, and fish likewise.

This is now the third time that Jesus shewed Himself to his disciples after that He was risen from the dead.

¶ So when they had dined, Jesus saith to Simon Peter, Simon, *son* of Jonas, lovest thou me more than these? He saith unto Him, Yea, Lord; thou knowest that I love thee. He saith unto him, Feed my lambs.

He saith to him again the second time, Simon, *son* of Jonas, lovest thou me? He saith unto Him, Yea, Lord; thou knowest that I love thee. He saith unto Him, Feed my sheep.

He saith unto him the third time, Simon, *son* of Jonas, lovest thou me? Peter was grieved because he said unto him the third time, Lovest thou me? And he said unto Him, Lord thou knowest all things; thou knowest that I love thee. Jesus saith

And he said unto Him, Lord, Thou knowest all things; Thou knowest that I love Thee.

unto him, Feed my sheep.

Verily, verily, I say unto thee, When thou wast young, thou girdest thyself and walkedst whither thou wouldest: but when thou shalt be old, thou shalt stretch forth thy hands, and another shall gird thee, and carry *thee* whither thou wouldest not.

This spake He, signifying by what death He should glorify God. And when He had spoken this, He saith unto him, Follow me.

Then Peter, turning about, seeth the disciple whom Jesus loved following; which also leaned on His breast at supper, and said, Lord, which is he that betrayeth thee?

Peter seeing him saith to Jesus, Lord, and what *shall* this man *do?*

Jesus saith unto him, If I will that he tarry till I come, what *is that* to thee? follow thou me.

Then went this saying abroad among the brethren, that that disciple should not die: yet Jesus said not unto him, He shall not die; but, If I will that he tarry till I come, what *is that* to thee?

This is the disciple which testifieth of these things, and wrote these things: and we know that his testimony is true.

¶ Then the eleven disciples went away into Galilee, into a mountain where Jesus had appointed them.

(After that, He was seen of above five hundred brethren at once.)

And when they saw Him, they worshipped Him: but some doubted.

And Jesus came and spake unto them, saying, All power is given unto me in heaven and in earth.

Go ye therefore, and teach all nations, baptizing them in the name of the Father, and of the Son, and of the Holy Ghost;

Teaching them to observe all things whatsoever I have commanded you: and, lo, I am with you always, *even* unto the end of the world.

After that, He was seen of James; then of all the apostles; to whom also He shewed Himself alive after His passion by many infallible proofs, being seen of them forty days, and speaking of the things pertaining to the kingdom of God:

And, being assembled together with *them*, commanded them that they should not depart from Jerusalem, but wait for the promise of the Father, which, *saith* He, ye have heard of me.

For John truly baptized with water; but ye shall be baptized with the Holy Ghost not many days hence.

When they therefore were come together they asked of Him, saying, Lord, wilt thou at this time restore again the kingdom to Israel?

And He said unto them, It is not for you to know the times or the seasons, which the Father hath put in His own power.

But ye shall receive power, after that the Holy Ghost is come upon you: and ye shall be witnesses unto me both in Jerusalem and in all Judea, and in Samaria, and unto the uttermost part of the earth.

And behold, I send the promise of my Father upon you: but tarry ye in the

And it came to pass, while He blessed them, He was parted from them, and carried up into heaven.

city of Jerusalem, until ye be endued with power from on high.

¶ And He led them out as far as to Bethany, and He lifted up His hands and blessed them.

And while He blessed them, He was parted from them, and while they beheld, He was taken up into heaven, and a cloud received Him out of their sight.

And while they looked steadfastly toward heaven as He went up, behold, two men stood by them in white apparel;

Which also said, Ye men of Galilee, why stand ye gazing up into heaven? this same Jesus, which is taken up from you into heaven, shall so come in like manner as ye have seen Him go into heaven.

And they worshiped Him and returned to Jerusalem with great joy;

And were continually in the temple, praising and blessing God.

¶ And many other signs truly did Jesus in the presence of His d i s c i p l e s, which are not written in this book;

But these are written, that ye might believe that Jesus is the Christ, the Son of God; and that believing, ye might have life through His name.

And they went forth, and preached every where, the Lord w o r k i n g with *t h e m*, a n d confirming the word with signs following.

The appearances of the Lord Jesus, after His ascension, as recorded by Luke in the VII and IX chapters of the "Acts of the Apostles."

TO STEPHEN.

But he, being full of the Holy G h o s t, looked up steadfastly into heaven, and saw the glory of God, and Jesus standing on the right hand of God.

And said, Behold, I see the heavens opened, and the Son of man standing on the right hand of God.

And they stoned Stephen, calling upon *God*, and saying, Lord Jesus receive my spirit.

And he kneeled down and cried with a loud voice, Lord, lay not this sin to their charge. And when he had said this, he fell asleep. And Saul was consenting unto his death.

TO SAUL.

And as he journeyed, he came near Damascus: and suddenly there shined round about him a light from heaven:

And he fell to the earth, and heard a voice saying unto him, Saul, Saul, why persecutest thou me?

And he said, Who art thou Lord? And the Lord said, I am Jesus whom thou persecutest.

"Behold, I see the heavens opened, and the Son of man standing on the right hand of God."

"And last of all He was seen of me also, as of one born out of due time."

"Jesus Christ is passing by."

www.ingramcontent.com/pod-product-compliance
Lightning Source LLC
Chambersburg PA
CBHW051234300426
44114CB00011B/737